ANDREA F. PHILLIPS

PLINIO

A Man for Our Times

THE AMERICAN SOCIETY FOR THE DEFENSE
OF TRADITION, FAMILY AND PROPERTY—TFP
SPRING GROVE, PA. 17362

Copyright © 2010 The American Society for the Defense of
Tradition, Family and Property®—TFP®
1358 Jefferson Road
Spring Grove, PA 17362
Tel.: (888) 317-5571
www.TFP.org

Design: Elizabeth Ferraz

The American Society for the Defense of Tradition, Family and
Property® and TFP® are registered names of The Foundation for a
Christian Civilization, Inc., a 501(c)(3) tax-exempt organization.

ISBN-10: 1-877905-42-9
ISBN-13: 978-1-877905-42-1
Library of Congress Control Number: 2010934817

Printed in the USA

"When still very young
I marveled at the ruins of Christendom,
Gave them my heart,
Turned my back on all I could expect,
And made of that past full of blessings,
My future."

—*Plinio Corrêa de Oliveira*

I dedicate this book to my father, to my husband, to my two brothers, and to a host of spiritual brothers, men in whom I was given to know and admire unabashed Catholic manhood, and who, along with Professor Plinio, inspired this work.

CONTENTS

FOREWORD

This book is not intended to be a complete biography of a personality as rich as Professor Plinio Corrêa de Oliveira's, especially as there is already a more extensive and scholarly work in English, written by Prof. Roberto de Mattei, a brilliant Italian intellectual, titled *The Crusader of the 20th Century: Plinio Corrêa de Oliveira.*

While strictly accurate from the standpoint of historical fact, this unpretentious work is intended to highlight aspects of Plinio Corrêa de Oliveira's unique personality in a light style, presenting, as it were, a series of frescoes of his exceptional life.

God is admirable in His holy and righteous men. Without preempting in any way the judgment of the Church, the fact is that no one can learn about a life such as Plinio Corrêa de Oliveira's without admiring God even more.

For me, writing this book—in spite of the arduous and laborious work of putting it together as happens with any such project—has been a source of great consolation and spiritual enrichment. If the reader should benefit from it in like manner, I will feel greatly rewarded.

Ut in omnibus glorificetur Deus.
That in all things God may be glorified.

May 13, 2010
A.F.P.

Chapter 1
Plinio

"The more intense the evils of an epoch, the more exceptional are the figures Divine Providence calls to face them. It is a reflection of His design to fight crises, calling souls of fire."

—Cardinal Bernardino Echeverría Ruiz

The young man stepped up to the podium and faced half a million upturned faces.

Chosen to deliver the closing address to the civil and religious authorities at the solemn Eucharistic Congress of 1942 in São Paulo, Brazil, the young Catholic leader spoke from the heart, dazzling his audience with his inspired eloquence. Time and again, he was interrupted by thunderous applause.

Plinio delivers a speech during the Fourth Eucharistic Congress in São Paulo, Brazil in September, 1942.

". . .Leaders of our nation, explore the riches of our soil; pattern our civil institutions after the maxims of the Church, the essence of Christian Civilization. Support the Holy Church of God in every way you can, so it may shape the national soul according to grace. . . Make Brazil a prosperous, organized and dynamic nation, and the Church will make Brazilians a great people. . ."[1]

As he closed, the multitude chanted in unison, "Plinio! Plinio! Plinio!"

At thirty-four, Plinio Corrêa de Oliveira was one of the
foremost Catholic lay leaders of Brazil, then the largest
Catholic nation on earth.

Having been elected deputy to the Federal Constitutional Assembly at age twenty-four with the largest number
of votes ever recorded, he helped guide his country in a
more godly direction. He dedicated his life to the service
of the Church and Christian Civilization and eventually
founded one of the most active anticommunist organizations of Catholic inspiration in the world, the Brazilian Society for the Defense of Tradition, Family and Property.

His was a life of dedication, sacrifice and combat
against the powers of evil in all their present manifestations, which earned one of his books the encomium of "a
most faithful echo of the documents of the Supreme Magisterium of the Church"[2] from the Holy See's Congregation

Plinio's mother, Lucilia Ribeiro dos Santos, in her mid-thirties posing for
a picture during a visit to Paris before World War I.

for Catholic Education, and
that of "Crusader of the 20th
Century" from his biographer,
Prof. Roberto de Mattei.

Certainly an exceptional
man, Divine Providence en-
dowed Plinio with the talents
and gifts that allowed him to
see clearly, step securely and
lead effectively, in the struggle for the Kingdom of Christ
on earth.

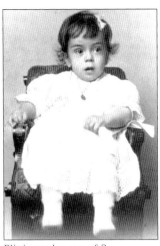

As he spoke that Septem-
ber 7, 1942, his eyes often

Plinio at the age of 2.

rested on a silver-haired lady, hands folded on her lap,
erect yet relaxed, dressed with perfect taste, her face at
once serious and sweet. She missed not a word that fell
from his lips and eyed him with a mixture of tenderness,
pride and vigilance. She was his mother. Even here, before this multitude, she had a way of evoking the journey
that brought him to where he stood. Only she and he
knew all it had entailed.

Beginnings

"Mamma, Mamma."

The three-year-old had clambered atop his sleeping
mother while his small hands pried open her eyelids.

At the relentless prodding, the eyes quivered then opened
revealing chestnut irises that softened in recognition.

"Oh, my son," she caressed the little one.

"Mamma, I woke up, it was dark, I was scared."

"You were scared? Oh, no. . . Mamma will tell you a story."

Plinio's parents, Dr. João Paulo Corrêa de Oliveira and Dona Lucilia Ribeiro dos Santos. They were married on July 15, 1906.

A while later the escapee was fast asleep as his mother laid him back in his own bed. There was an expression of infinite tenderness on her face as she contemplated her son before tiptoeing away to resume her own rest.

"What was that?" rumbled her husband.

"That was Plinio."

* * *

Plinio remembered his mother as the first light of his life. In fact her name, Lucilia, means "small light."

Lucilia Ribeiro dos Santos was born in 1876 in São Paulo, Brazil, then a constitutional monarchy. She was the daughter of a prominent lawyer, and the granddaughter of a brilliant politician. Her father also owned a coffee plantation, as did many of the families of like professionals in São Paulo. Her husband, João Paulo Corrêa de Oliveira was the son of sugar mill lords from the northeastern part of the country. Lucilia was thirty years old when she married the northern lawyer practicing in São Paulo. His uncle João Alfredo Corrêa de Oliveira, had been Minister and Councilor to the Empire, and an important player in obtaining the abolition of slavery in Brazil in 1888.

Their first child was a daughter, Rosée, and their second, Plinio, was born on December 13, 1908 when Lucilia was thirty-two. Her doctor had informed her that the birth could be risky and had suggested an abortion.

"Doctor," she retorted, "this is not a question a mother should be asked! It shouldn't even have crossed your mind."

Later, Plinio would say of her, "she was dignity without wealth, sweetness without cowardice, intransigence without rigidity, and nobility without arrogance."[3]

And though having received an eminently European formation, she was none the less thoroughly Brazilian.

"My homeland has many palm-trees and the thrush-song fills its air. . ."

To understand Plinio and his family, it is essential for the reader to capture something of their environment and surroundings, and that is, Brazil.

In 1500 as a Portuguese ship on its way to India wandered west from its southerly course, the captain, Pedro Alvarez Cabral, found himself peering at a lush coastline unknown to Europeans. The discoverers planted a cross in the white sand, and claimed the new territory for the king of Portugal. The chaplain offered Holy Mass on a makeshift altar, and the new country was named Land of the Holy Cross. Later it was renamed, Brazil, after the abundant Brazil wood.

Brazil was christened Catholic and adopted the language of its colonists, Portuguese.

After a government was established in 1549, the newly founded Jesuits arrived to begin a work of evangelization which was "unparalleled in history."[4]

Two towering figures in this monumental task were Fathers Manuel da Nóbrega, and Blessed José de Anchieta whose works and miracles fill vast chronicles. Much of the catechetical, moral, spiritual and educational formation of Brazil is historically attributed to these heroes. Under an able civil leadership and holy religious influence, the new country prospered.

In 1821 Pedro IV, son of King John VI of Portugal, was named the first resident regent of that enormous colony. The following year he proclaimed the independence of Brazil from Portugal and became its first emperor as Pedro I. His son succeeded him as Pedro II in 1840 and had a long and prosperous reign. Pedro II's daughter, Isabel, a pious, benevolent princess, granted freedom to the slaves in 1888. In 1889, a republican coup deposed the Emperor and exiled him and his family. Brazil became a republic.

This immense territory encompasses nearly one half of South America. Brazil's topography varies between great mountains, majestic shorelines, a rich fluvial system and lush vegetation. The luminosity of its atmosphere has been the inspiration of writers and poets alike.

> "In no other region is the sky as serene, nor the dawn more beautiful; in no other hemisphere are the sun's rays more golden, nor the moonlight reflections more brilliant. . . the horizons, whether at sunrise or at sunset, are always clear; the waters, whether from springs in the countryside or from the aqueducts of the towns, are the most pure; in short, Brazil is terrestrial paradise rediscovered."[5]

Brazil is the largest country in South America and, excluding Alaska, it is larger in territory than the United States. Brazil's population is 198 million.

As for the people of Brazil, they inherited the affectionate, contemplative soul of their Portuguese ancestors, along with a solid common sense and sincere goodness. Theirs is a universal outlook with the capacity of appreciating and assimilating the best of other cultures. To this national "personality" is added the intuition of the Indian and the natural good will of the black race. The affectionate, Catholic character of the Portuguese easily assimilated both the Indian and black populations, uniting all three races in one nation and one Faith.

Brazilians love their country and speak of it as a person. They hardly ever leave it and, when obliged to live abroad, they sing of it nostalgically, as Antonio Gonçalves Dias did in his famous 1843 poem:

> "My homeland has many palm-trees and the thrush-song fills its air; no bird here can sing as well as the birds sing over there."[6]

São Paulo

The Brazilian also has the industrious nature of the Portuguese, a healthy share of which was inherited by the na-

São Paulo, where Plinio was born, is one of the largest cities in the world with a metropolitan population of almost 19 million.

tives of São Paulo, the city where Plinio was born.

While Rio de Janeiro was the governmental capital of the country, São Paulo was soon to become its industrial center.

In 1908, the year of Plinio's birth, the city only numbered one hundred and fifty thousand inhabitants and was still under the influence of the last echoes of the "Belle Epoque" and bathed in the last glimmers of Victorian splendor and its "Sweetness of Living."

That "Sweetness of Living" was a reflection of Faith and Divine Love that still permeated a civilization inspired by Christ in a society that, at least exteriorly, was still devoted to God.

Good music, fine art, beautiful fashions, and the art of conversation requiring grace, civility, amiability and diplomacy were the social expression of this spirit that "sweetened" all of life.

At that time, Paris, the "city of light," was the acknowledged capital of that ideal world extending its frontiers well beyond France and Europe.

São Paulo, Brazil, was "one of the cities that best knew how to integrate the values of its traditions with those of French culture."[7]

On the other hand, as the "real bearers of the national energy,"[8] in a few decades the people of São Paulo were to transform the small cultured town into the largest industrial metropolis of the country.

This was the ambiance in which Plinio was born, lived and died.

Notes:

1. Plinio Corrêa de Oliveira, "Saudação às autoridades civis e militares," *O Legionário*, Sept. 7, 1942, http://www.pliniocorreadeoliveira.info/ DIS%20-%201942-09-07%20-%20IV%20Congresso%20Eucaristico.htm

2. Letter from Cardinal Giuseppe Pizzardo, Prefect of the Sacred Congregation of Seminaries and Universities and Dino Staffa, Secretary later made Cardinal regarding Plinio Corrêa de Oliveira's work "The Church and the Communist State: the Impossible Coexistence."

3. Plinio Corrêa de Oliveira, Meeting at São Paulo Apostolo center, February 2, 1982.

4. Roberto de Mattei, *The Crusader of the 20th Century: Plinio Corrêa de Oliveira*, (Herefordshire, England: Gracewing, Fowler Wright Books, 1998) p. 6, n. 19.

5. Sebastião da Rocha Pita (1660-1738), *História da America Portuguesa*, in E. Werneck. Antologia Brasileira, (Rio de Janeiro: Livraria Francisco Alves, 1939), p. 210, apud Roberto de Mattei, *The Crusader of the 20th Century*, p. 4, n. 8.

6. Nelson Ascher, trans., Antonio Goncalves Dias, "The Song of Exile." http://old-poetry.com/opoem/122918-Antonio-Goncalves-Dias-The-Song-Of-Exile

7. Roberto de Mattei, *The Crusader of the 20th Century*, p. 3.

8. Stefan Zweig, *Brazil: Land of the Future*, (London: Cassell, 1942), pp. 212-213, apud Roberto de Mattei, *The Crusader of the 20th Century*, p. 11, n. 45).

Plinio with his elder sister, Rosée.

CHAPTER 2
Childhood

"Culture contains an invariable basic element,
the refinement of the human spirit."

—*Plinio Corrêa de Oliveira*

"Mais non! Ce n'est pas vrai! Il est un prêtre, c'est pas bien!"

"No, it's not true! He is a priest, it's not right!"

Four-year-old Plinio stood on a chair at the Théâtre des Marionettes, his small body tense, his finger up in the air, arguing with a puppet alligator about to eat a marionette priest.

For several months now, the small boy and his family had been traveling in Europe. Dona[1] Lucilia suffered from gallstones, which were then only operated on by the pioneer Prof. August Bier, who was also personal doctor to Kaiser William II. She had sailed for Germany with her husband, two children and extended family in June of 1912. As trips to Europe were a special part in the cultural formation of Brazilian elites, they stayed until March of 1913. After convalescing at the baths of Binz, and visiting Wiesbaden and Cologne, the family spent the winter in Paris.

It was there that small Plinio had several encounters with the marionettes in the Champs-Elysées Gardens. This spectacle of a Brazilian boy arguing morality in French[2] drew a larger crowd than usual. Suspiciously enough, the marionettes went on a tirade of bad behavior, which kept Plinio climbing on his chair and the ticket booth busy.

One day, Dona Lucilia took Rosée and Plinio to the famous pastry and candy shop, Marquise de Sévigné. After the children had chosen a sweet, the lady behind the counter packaged them beautifully and handed each a parcel. Plinio immediately took possession of his and made his way to the door. The sooner he arrived at the hotel to do justice to this delicious treat, the better.

"Plinio," said his mother, "why don't you offer to carry your sister's box as a gentleman should?"

The lad immediately acquiesced, and now, holding a package in each hand, walked resolutely down the street with his mother and sister.

Just then, a distinguished gentleman approached, and making a sign to Dona Lucilia not to worry, stepped directly in front of Plinio and snatching the two parcels exclaimed,

"Thank you very much, Sir, you are so kind to give me

Plinio in Paris at the age of 4.

these!" and turned to go.

Plinio's reaction was spontaneous. He rushed after him and hanging on to one of his legs began in his strong voice,

"Sir! Give me back our parcels! You have committed two sins. You've lied by saying I gave these to you—and I didn't. And you've stolen, taking what is not yours!"

The man laughed and returned the borrowed goods, while tipping his hat to Dona Lucilia.

"Ma'am, congratulations on your boy. I have often watched him debate at the Théâtre des Marionettes and could not resist teasing him."

She smiled and acknowledged the compliment, inwardly pleased at her son's rectitude and courage.

As Dona Lucilia was still recuperating, the children's Nanny often took Plinio for a walk through the parks of Paris. One day, a distinguished couple approached them, and introduced themselves as Polish Counts. After an amiable conversation, they asked the boy if he would like to live with them in their castle in Poland.

Plinio's big brown eyes glittered at the mention of a "castle," but then grew serious,

"Would my mother come?"

On receiving a negative answer, his own was swift,

"Then I don't go either."

The amused Counts went on their way, but every time they met the pair on such promenades, they asked again,

"So, my young lad, how about coming with us to our castle?"

"Only if my mother comes," was the resolute response.

After a few of these encounters, Nanny thought it wise to inform Dona Lucilia of them. Concerned, she made it a point to meet the couple on the next outing. They soon crossed paths, and after the first pleasantries, the couple told Dona Lucilia of their usual "proposal" to Plinio and his non-negotiable condition, congratulating her on her son's love and devotion.

A "sense of the marvelous"

"I'm not going. I want to buy this place and live here," announced small Plinio to his wide eyed, slightly amused parents, as he clung to the golden wheel of a royal carriage in Versailles.

"Plinio," his father's voice was stern, "come away from that wheel," and took him in his arms.

Plinio was always too intelligent not to know when he lost a battle, and did not resist.

As his mother led him away by the hand, his big brown eyes swept once more over that "marvelous" vehicle, and as they walked, took in once more that wonderful palace and gardens, the stuff of which dreams were made.

From an early age Plinio was attracted to the marvelous, lofty and beautiful aspects of life as handed down by tradition, which he later called "the sense of the marvelous or beauty." Later in life he was to understand that the contemplation of beauty is one of the ways that leads the soul to God.

Growing up in a world where not only truth and goodness were to be systematically attacked, but also the beauty of life consistently stripped, Plinio was to become not only a champion of truth and goodness, but of beauty as well. All his life he would see beauty, decorum and good taste as concomitant with goodness and truth, and essential factors in the upbringing of children.

The family trip to Europe was his first introduction to that marvelous world of old Christendom, that civilization steeped in the "sweet odor of Our Lord Jesus Christ."[3]

Despite his young age, he captured the sublime meaning of all he saw and experienced such as the Cathedral of Cologne, the castles speckled along the Rhine, Notre Dame and the Sainte Chapelle in Paris, and the golden carriages at Versailles. His enthusiasm knew no bounds when he witnessed a troop of French Cuirassiers in their golden helmets and breastplates. To him these men hovered somewhere between earth and heaven, and to his manly heart the "marvelous" was never so wonderful as when arrayed for battle. He was also attracted by the charms of European folklore, and by all that was true, good and beautiful in Christian culture, which he saw as the influence of the personality of Our Lord Jesus Christ, at once regal and humble, majestic and accessible, grandiose and full of charm. He loved that civilization and made it his own.

Many years later on another visit to the Cathedral of Cologne, he was to say after contemplating the grandeur and perfection of its Gothic architecture,

> "[It is] something mysterious that calls for my full dedication and enthusiasm; that urges my soul to be in full conformity with the marvels of the Catholic Church!
>
> "It is a school of thought, will and sensibility.
>
> "A way of being is derived from it, for which I feel I was born. It is something much greater than I and which comes from long before my time. It is something that comes from centuries ago when I was nothing. It comes from the Catholic mentality of men who preceded me and who also had, deep in their souls, this same desire for the unimaginable."[4]

"Fräulein"

Plinio who had spoken his first words at six months, continued to show signs of a precocious intellect.

After their trip to Europe, Dona Lucilia engaged the services of the German governess Mathilde Heldmann.

Fräulein Mathilde, as the children called her, was a native of Regensburg, a Bavarian town, and had worked for families of the European nobility. Plinio always considered the hiring of such a qualified governess as one of the best things their parents did for his sister and for himself. Not only did both profit from her positive

Fräulein Mathilde Heldmann, Rosée and Plinio's governess, was from Bavaria.

Germanic discipline, but also from her love of order and beauty as she spoke to them of that slowly fading world of the European Belle Époque with all its decorum, ceremony, manners and good taste. A superb teacher and great storyteller, "Fräulein" was vital in Plinio's formation, also teaching him and his sister German and English in which they became fluent.

Sowing the seeds of Faith

Along with the tendency to see God in all that is wonderful and beautiful in Creation, Plinio saw the religious intertwined in all aspects of Christian Civilization, and his attraction for it grew.

He credited his mother with fostering religion in his heart as she pointed to the statues of the Sacred Heart of Jesus and the Immaculate Heart of Mary even before teaching him to say Papai and Mamãe.[5] He was to say later, "My mother taught me to love Our Lord Jesus Christ, she taught me to love the Holy Catholic Church."[6]

The devotion to the Sacred Heart of Jesus was Dona Lucilia's favorite. Not far from their home, there was a beautiful church dedicated to the Sacred Heart of Jesus where she went every day with her children. It was here, watching his mother in prayer, that Plinio understood the source of her piety and goodness, "I perceived that her way of being came from her devotion to the Sacred Heart of Jesus, through Our Lady."

Thus Plinio's upbringing was a mixture of European culture and Brazilian good sense, aristocratic manners and Germanic discipline, tempered by a simple, solid Faith.

His love of the Church and Christendom was later to inspire one of his most beautiful lines,

> "When still very young
> I marveled at the ruins of Christendom,
> gave them my heart,
> turned my back on all I could expect,
> and made of that past full of blessings,
> my future."[7]

Notes:
    1. "Dona" is the Portuguese equivalent of the Southern "Miss" used for both single and married ladies, as in "Miss Daisy." It is a way of showing deference without the formality of the "Miss" or "Mrs." followed by the last name. It is a contraction of Domina, Lady.
    2. Plinio had begun to pick up French by listening to the conversations of the adults around the family table. He loved the language and later spoke it like his own.
    3. Plinio's usual expression at many conferences and talks.
    4. Plinio Corrêa de Oliveira, "O inimaginável e o sonhado," *Catolicismo*, no. 543, Mar. 1996, http://www.catolicismo.com.br/materia/materia.cfm/idmat/01C00D09-3048-560B-1CC4FBD7A32FCE58/mes/Março1996.
    5. "Pappa" and "Mamma" or "Daddy" and "Mommy" in Portuguese.
    6. Roberto de Mattei, *The Crusader of the Twentieth Century*, pp. 16-17.
    7. John R. Spann and José Aloisio A. Schelini, trans., António A. Borelli Machado, coord., *Tradition Family Property: Half a Century of Epic Anticommunism*, (Pleasantville, N.Y., The Foundation for a Christian Civilization, Inc., 1981), frontispiece.

Plinio and his sister Rosée in Spanish costume during a family celebration in the city of Santos, the largest seaport in the state of São Paulo.

CHAPTER 3
Growing Up in a Changing World

"Almost suddenly, under the impulse of mysterious factors, everything began to change..."

—*Um Homem, uma Obra, uma Gesta*

As Plinio's father was from the north of Brazil but practiced in São Paulo, Plinio grew up mostly around his mother's family, the Ribeiro dos Santos, one of the most traditional families in the region.

At that time there was much talk about the political situation of Brazil. Many families, loyal to the old monarchy, were still advocates of that system.

Some republicans were anti-clerical and hoped for a government with socialistic leanings, not so much for their own days but for those of their grandchildren. The so-called "bold spirits" were found even in a family as traditional as the Ribeiro dos Santos. At family reunions, they invariably flaunted their atheism and aired their socialist opinions against those of their devout Catholic relatives, though always holding to the good manners of the time.

Plinio, now a growing boy, missed nothing of those talks, and soon noticed that while the "bold spirits" dominated the conversations as heralds of a "better future," the practicing Catholics and supporters of tradition often appeared confused and on the defensive.[1]

Though Dona Lucilia did not participate in the debates, her heart was full of love for Brazil's more Christian past. Plinio followed her lead and rejected any entreaties to take a position contrary to his inclinations, consistently championing the cause of tradition.

In the throes of change

The period after World War I was one of rapid transformation for Brazil. The rise of Communism in Russia and the unrest that spread throughout Central Europe sent ripples all the way to São Paulo, where street demonstrations and labor conflicts often turned violent. The social and cultural atmosphere of São Paulo changed, and much of the splendor and glitter of the Belle Époque began to wane.

Rapid mechanization favored this process. Already São Paulo was entering the dizzying industrial boom that would transform the small, pleasant city of the twenties into the largest industrial hub of South America.

The budding feminist movement and the "Hollywood syndrome"

On the other hand, the budding feminist movement, the promotion of masculine fashions for women, and the introduction of more casual manners also contributed to that "brave new world" that Plinio increasingly opposed.

And then there was the cinema. Already fascinated with the first tarmacked highways, the first radio stations and first airplanes, people were riveted by the movies. Hollywood films enthralled the multitudes and proclaimed the post-war changes irreversible. In the euphoria of peace, prosperity and progress, almost everyone was swept along by this "liberalizing" current and gave no thought to the bitter consequences that process would bring throughout the course of the century.

Plinio would later recall:

> "That decade (the twenties) was a 'life of idleness,' of fabulous expenditures, of high coffee bean prices, of constant trips to Europe, of or-

gies and a carefree life. . . The mental stagnation of Brazilians was total. The famous jazz band, the shimmy, cinema, and sports monopolized everyone's mind."[2]

A young thinker

Just as Plinio's large intelligent eyes had taken in the remnants of European Christian Civilization and fallen in love with them, offering his first defense of that world at the Théâtre des Marionettes, he now watched a new "cultural revolution" and decided he did not like it. Amazingly mature for his age, he was already a thinker and analyzer of events. With the help of a strong Faith, his

Plinio during his school days at Colégio São Luís.

precocious mind separated the wheat from the chaff with surprising ease. This would be his life-long charisma, to diagnose the errors of the times, even the most subliminal, as opposed to the truths of the Kingdom of Christ on earth.

School

In 1919, when Plinio was ten years old, his parents enrolled him in the Colégio São Luís of the Jesuit Fathers, the school where the sons of São Paulo's ruling class were educated.

At the Colégio São Luís, Plinio learned to love the spirit of Saint Ignatius Loyola, an important factor in his formation. He was attracted to the seriousness, depth and consistency of the method, which teaches and invites souls to practice the Faith to its fullest. Here, Plinio found a continuation to Dona Lucilia's religious influence, as well as logical elements to further deepen and mature his Catholic conviction, now budding into enthusiastic love. From then on, Plinio began to attend religious practices and frequent the Sacraments more assiduously.

Plinio on the day of his First Communion.

First battlefield

On the other hand, school was for young Plinio his first clash with the world, and his first battlefield.

At the Colégio São Luís he felt the shock of an atmosphere vastly different from that of his family, an atmosphere at once respectful, affectionate, pure and lofty. He soon found that the students were already caught up in the "Hollywood" mentality penetrating Brazilian life. For Plinio's classmates, the word "American" enclosed a simplistic, false image of the true United States, which Hollywood projected abroad, and which no Brazilian schoolboy questioned. That mentality spelled modernity, dynamism, self-realization, pragmatism, contempt for culture and reflection, enthusiasm for agitation and adventure, egalitarianism and sensuality.

Plinio also encountered the spirit of impurity, adopted by many a boy, and clearly perceived its link to a form of atheism and egalitarianism. He noticed that the students who told dirty jokes and engaged in obscene conversations were also irreligious, vulgar and hostile to noble values. On the other hand, he saw that the true spirit of Saint Ignatius as taught by the Jesuit Fathers upheld morality, religion, discipline, good manners, and lofty customs.

Now he faced the same challenge in his peers as posed by the "bold spirits" at home. Either Plinio would resist or he would yield to changes that his soul rejected. He looked for like-minded colleagues but found none.

Rather than offering a Quixotic opposition to everything and everyone, Plinio adopted a tactical approach. He chose to remain faithful to the convictions maturing in his soul and never say or do anything contrary to them.

However, he would voice his views only on those occasions

when he judged he had a chance of prevailing in an argument. Like every serious fighter, Plinio was learning strategy.

Drawing large conclusions

It was at the Colégio São Luis that Plinio understood that the battle for or against God and His Church is the most important thing in life. It is by fidelity to this Church, the world is given the means to secure its best ideals to a firm rock, and reject all error and evil. On the contrary, if the world rejects God and His Church, social customs, institutions, peoples and civilizations inevitably head for destruction. The new order of things all around him, based on secularism, was empty, inconsistent and doomed to failure.

He realized that only Christian Civilization is capable of producing an order of things that can inspire and sustain authentic progress, a progress that is at once tempered and fair, and diametrically different from the crazed gallop towards pleasure and prosperity that the new order had launched.

In Plinio's twelve-year-old soul, these convictions had already become rock solid, as he thought,

> "Whatever happens to me, I will oppose this [new] world. This world and I are irreconcilable. I will fight for purity, for the Church and for an aristocratic society,[3] and I will stand up for hierarchy, decorum and manners even if I become the last of men, stepped on and ostracized. These values and I are one, and regardless of what others choose, this will be my life."[4]

Many a time, young Plinio faced the option of either selling out to his environment, to all those who represented 'modernity,' and become impure, irreligious and vulgar or he would find a way to rally those who did not want to change but rather to project into the future the dynamism of a holy tradition and start a Crusade.

In his young soul a resolve was maturing: to place his talents, his gifts and his life at the service of Christian Civilization, in whatever manner God might choose.

Notes:

1. Regarding the various forms of government, namely, monarchy, aristocracy and democracy, the Church teaches that "each of them is good, provided it lead straight to its end—that is to say, to the common good for which social authority is constituted." Pope Leo XIII, Encyclical Au milieu des sollicitudes, Feb. 16, 1892, no. 14, in Claudia Carlen, I.H.M., The Papal Encyclicals 1878-1903, (n.c.: McGrath Publishing Company, 1981), p. 280.

2. Plinio Corrêa de Oliveira, "A dinamite de Cristo," O Legionário, Nov. 5, 1938, http://www.pliniocorreadeoliveira.info/LEG%20381105_AdinamitedeCristo.

3. Plinio believed in the power of true, duty-bound, God-fearing elites to inspire and raise up the culture of nations. He expounds brilliantly on this subject in his book, Nobility and Analogous Traditional Elites in the Allocutions of Pius XII.

4. Marcos Machado, ed., Plinio Corrêa de Oliveira, Memórias dos Anos 50, (mimeograph), p. 44.

CHAPTER 4
Beginnings of Devotion to Mary

"Save me, O Queen, Mother of Mercy, our life,
our sweetness and our hope…"

—*Young Plinio*

"Son, what is this?" Dona Lucilia's eyes were serious as she inspected Plinio's monthly report card. There were watermarks all over the page, and on the slot corresponding to "Good Demeanor" in Geography class there was a blotchy 100 in his own handwriting.

Plinio could not lie, much less to his mother. He looked into her questioning eyes and confessed,

"They gave me a sixty for behavior and I knew you wouldn't like it, so I changed the grade. It was too obvious so I let the rain fall on it trying to blotch it, but it fell everywhere else instead."

Her eyes, normally a light chestnut darkened.

"My son a forger?! NEVER!"

Plinio never forgot her horror at what he had done. The contrast between her unfailing sweetness and this unbending severity was chastening.

He had not deserved that grade. He knew he was well behaved in class. There had been a mistake. But he also knew good behavior was more important to his mother than academic achievement. She often said,

"No one can help it if they are not intelligent. But everyone can be expected to behave. I will not tolerate misbehavior."

These words, added to the fact that he had played a few boyish pranks lately, led him to "doctor up" his report card in the hopes of evading unpleasantness. To make matters worse, there was another more recent mischief she did not even know about, and if she found out...

"I will have to speak of these things to your father. If you continue on this path, we may have to send you to Caraça," her voice brought him back with a jolt.

Caraça! Oh, no! That was a far-away boarding school, practically a reformatory. If he went to Caraça he would not see his family and beloved mother for a whole year.

"Save me, O Queen!"

That Sunday, as he knelt in one of the pews on the right-hand nave of the Church of the Sacred Heart, his eyes were fixed on the statue of Mary Help of Christians. A storm raged in his heart, and he prayed with all his soul, "Save me, O Queen!"

Statue of Our Lady Help of Christians in the church of the Sacred Heart of Jesus in São Paulo, before which young Plinio prayed during his troubles over his report card.

Thus he began the Hail Holy Queen. In Portuguese, "Hail" is "Salve," which can also mean "save me." Ignorant of the first meaning, he took the second as most appropriate for his plight, as he felt lost.

Years later he recounted that as he prayed, without a vision or revelation of any kind, he had the strong impression that the statue was looking at him tenderly, promising him protection not only for that moment but for all of his life.

There and then he knew that with Our Lady, no matter what he did, as long as he was willing to acknowledge it, he would always be delivered. He also understood that regardless of his failings, she would always obtain forgiveness for him from her Divine Son.

He asked her to protect him, to make him a pure young man, and a true Catholic.

He left with the feeling that she would mend it all.

Dona Lucilia did speak with Dr. João Paulo, and both agreed he would call on Father Dréneuf, principal of Colégio São Luiz. After checking the records, Father Dréneuf verified the mistake. Plinio's true grade was indeed 100. The storm passed with no more mention of Caraça.

That day, a deep filial attachment to Mary Most Holy was born in Plinio's heart. This devotion would be the guiding star of his life, the fountain from which he would draw his courage and strength.

CHAPTER 5
Law School and Inklings of Another Vocation

"Our Lord Jesus Christ, the ineffable personification of all perfection, is the embodiment, the sublime model, the focus, vigor, life, glory, standard and delight of true culture."

—*Plinio Corrêa de Oliveira*

At the age of seventeen, following family tradition, Plinio Corrêa de Oliveira enrolled in the famed Law School of the University of São Paulo. Its faculty was secularist and its student body, for the most part, had the same "Hollywood" mentality of many of the students of the Colégio São Luis, only advanced in time and age. In all, the university was considered a bulwark of secularism. It was the year 1926.

Though applying himself seriously to his law studies, Plinio continued cultivating his philosophical, moral and spiritual life. One of the books he read during this period was *The Soul of the Apostolate* by Dom Jean-Baptiste Chautard. This book, a lifelong favorite of Plinio's, was a precious antidote to the "heresy of action" then beginning to infect society.

The "heresy of action" came with the roaring twenties, preaching activism with little thought to the development of the interior life. On the contrary, Dom Chautard argued that every efficacious

Dom Jean-Baptiste Chautard, author of *The Soul of the Apostolate,* a book which greatly influenced Plinio throughout his life.

action, especially where apostolate is concerned, is rooted in one's interior life and in union with God. The inner life of a Catholic is the real powerhouse for his action.

Plinio, though dedicated to public action and the apostolate from a very young age, never neglected his prayer life and his spiritual development.

To restore all things in Christ

He believed with all his soul in the statement of Pope Leo XIII, "the whole human race is most truly under the power of Jesus Christ,"[1] and, in his heart, was aware of a calling mysteriously linked to the mission of the great Saint Pius X, "to restore all things in Christ."

Against the backdrop of budding Communism, Fascism and Hollywoodian Americanism, the young student felt called to work to help in this restoration, especially in temporal society.

A new order opposed to Christ's order

On the other hand, Plinio detected the machinations of a liberal tide that penetrated culture undermining faith and morals. The pursuit of money and unbridled pleasure was the word of the day. This liberal tide influenced all of society changing its customs, rules of interaction, music, dress code, architecture and therefore people's mentality. Like a pernicious gas, it was a slow, gentle, but powerful

Plinio with other students at the São Paulo Law School.

process. Because it was slow it did not alarm, and because it was gentle it did not awake.

All the while it made ever deeper inroads into the daily habits of people influencing their tendencies away from centuries-old Christian customs. These customs with their sweet austerity, discipline and sobriety had thus far promoted order and respect in a civilization illumined by the light of Christ.

A time for change

It was a time for radical changes.

Skirts, which had gone up from the floor to the ankles in the first decade of the century, now were poised for another lift to mid-calf. Women were exchanging the Gibson style for the "garçonne" look by sheering their tresses and wearing their hair close cropped, while men were leaving tails and top hats for the stripes and box hat.

It was all about "throwing out the old musty stuff" and letting in "the lighter air" of a carefree attitude. "Light" was the word of the day, applied to wardrobes, music and morals.

Plinio looked at all this with his analyzing eyes and said one day to a friend,

"I don't like these skirts going up. . ."

"Why, Plinio, there is nothing wrong! Ladies have plenty on. . . They just don't need all that fabric. . ."

"Watch," continued Plinio undeterred, "in a few decades, if we are still around, we are going to witness near nudism."

"Plinio! You are so exaggerated!"

Plinio was alive, and still drawing logical conclusions when the mini-skirt, and the first scandalous bikini came out.

Looking for answers in history and looking for the "others"

As a young boy, Plinio had a back condition that necessitated lying flat on the floor after lunch. To pass the time, he began to read a compilation of historical articles from a French encyclopedic book in his grandfather's library, all the while seeking to understand the Christian Civilization of old.

With time, as he delved deeper and deeper into the history of Christendom, slowly composing a picture of what that civilization had been, with its code of Christian morality and chivalry, hierarchical order and cultural richness, he began to ask what could be done to contain the wave of destruction advancing on all fronts. What could be done to renew in the world fidelity to the doctrines of the Church and traditions of the Christian West?

Plinio in military uniform in his late teens. The army afforded the young follower of Christ the time for vocational discernment as well as a protecting shield against the prevalent social corruption of the time.

Furthermore, by studying the French Revolution and the Russian Communist Revolution in depth, and by understanding what godlessness had wanted to destroy, he understood better what God had built. Using a method of contrast between good and evil, as darkness offsets the splendor of light, he arrived at an accurate idea of what Christian Civilization is meant to be and *had* been to a great extent.

All the while, his main point of reference was the Catholic Church. Later, this thought process would result in his masterpiece, the essay *Revolution and Counter-Revolution.*

Young Plinio longed to find others who thought like he. An inner voice promised those "others" would come.

Notes:
1. Leo XIII, Encyclical *Annum Sacrum*, May 25, 1899, no. 3, in Claudia Carlen, I.H.M., *The Papal Encyclicals 1878-1903*, (n.c., McGrath Publishing Company, 1981), p. 452, http://www.vatican.va/holy_father/leo_xiii/encyclicals/documents/hf_l-xiii_enc_25051899_annum-sacrum_en.html.

CHAPTER 6
Marian Congregation

*"The whole essence of a Christian life is to reject
the corruption of the world and to oppose
constantly any indulgence in it."*

—*Pope Leo XIII*

Where are the others? Plinio often asked himself. "True," he mused one day as he rode a tram through the streets of São Paulo, "I have met pious and prayerful young men. There must be some who besides being pious also see the perils that surround us, sense the slow undermining of Christian Civilization, and are willing to fight for the Kingdom of Christ."

Wait—they will come, a gentle inner voiced whispered.

As the tram passed a church, Plinio saw a large banner stretched across its façade. It read:

Catholic Youth Congress—September 9-16 (1928)

Plinio sat upright, head turning and eyes straining as the car rumbled by. In the large, bold banner he had sensed a spirited challenge to the anti-religious trend of the day. Here is militant Catholicism at last, he smiled. And he signed up.

On September 9, after asking his mother's usual blessing, nineteen-year-old Plinio eagerly made his way to the Monastery Church of Saint Benedict where the Congress convened. As he stepped into the courtyard, he could not believe his eyes and ears. There was a sea of enthusiastic young men, bubbling with the joy of meeting on a common ideal. For the young man who had so far fought alone, this was hope indeed. That week, he found "the others." There were several young men who thought and felt like he and who believed they could offer a united front to the neo-pagan wave invading society.

Plinio had found the Catholic Movement.

The Catholic Movement and the Marian Congregation

In the twenties and early thirties the religious climate in Brazil was still imbued with the beneficial action of Pope Saint Pius X and the results of his battle against Modernism. Brazil's clergy had men of valor and prestige, and was largely trusted and revered. Cardinal Se-bastião Leme of Rio de Janeiro, who succeeded Archbishop Cavalcanti, St. Pius X's appointee for Rio, became the recognized leader of the episcopate. And men such as São Paulo's Arch-bishop Duarte Leopoldo e Silva were a force to be reckoned with.

Such an ambiance gave rise to the Catholic Movement in Brazil com-prising many religious organizations some of which were extraordinarily vigorous. The Marian Congregation was one of the most dynamic. Practi-cally every parish hosted a chapter. This Marian Movement encompassed tens of thousands of men and women from all classes of society. From all corners of the country, the Marian Congregation had an extraordinary impulse, encouraging legions of youth to develop an interior life and an apostolic spirit. It was a true na-

Plinio as a young Marian Congregant.

tional force.

Shocking his world

On the other hand, the secularist movement spread like a pernicious gas with a large adhesion from the ruling class. So far, Plinio, because of his birth in an aristocratic family, had moved mostly in the circles of São Paulo's high society where it was fashionable to "shun" religion. Though the practice of the Faith was tolerated in women, it was deemed a weakness in men.

After the Catholic Youth Congress, Plinio officially joined the Marian Congregation of the parish of Saint Cecilia. The noon Mass was the one frequented by São Paulo's high society. One day, an astonished congregation watched as Plinio walked the Stations of the Cross, small blue rosary in hand.

"Can you believe it," whispered one lady to another, "That's Plinio 'walking' the way of the Cross!"

The other lady's eyes opened wide.

"And he has a light blue rosary in his hand. . ."

"Could at least be black," grumbled her husband beside her.

It was a scandal. Plinio knew it. But there he was, with his light blue rosary going from one station to the other before the whole congregation. He was not only fighting his own human respect but "breaking the ice" in his own circle. Later he confessed that he had purposely bought a light blue rosary just to cause ripples.

Gifted with intelligence, oratory and leadership, Plinio became one of the foremost leaders of the Marian Movement. He was soon to organize it at an unlikely place— his university.

Plinio during one of his many speeches as a Catholic leader. All of Plinio's speeches were delivered extemporaneously. He used notes only once for his very first speech.

CHAPTER 7
Young Lawyer and Catholic Leader

*"Times are coming and may already be here
when to be good will not be good enough. Man will
either have to be heroic or he will be a coward."*

—*Plinio Corrêa de Oliveira*

"There's the campus sacristan," joked one law student to his colleague pointing to Plinio standing at the campus gate distributing Catholic papers.

"Let's tease him," tittered the other as they approached the gate.

"Why, Plinio are you a sacristan now?"

"No, law student and militant Catholic," answered Plinio in his strong voice and positive manner, "never heard of the Marian Congregations? Where have you two been? Take a paper." Before they knew it, they both had a paper in their hand.

In 1929, in his third year of college, Plinio started a Catholic movement with four or five Marian Congregants at the Law School. They named their group University Catholic Action (UCA) and began publishing a paper on Catholic ideas and current news.

UCA members distributed the publications at different points of the university but Plinio set up shop at the "lion's mouth." As he boldly offered his paper at the gate, some turned it down fuming at the provocation.

How dare he, this is a secular establishment of learning, not a den of religious superstition, was written on many a scowl.

Others were more polite,

"Thanks," and turned it down with a wave of the hand.

Still, others timidly asked questions, which told Plinio that they would not mind professing their Faith but just did not dare in the hostile environment of the Law School.

With time, the members of the UCA grew in numbers and influence. In a few years the UCA was to spread to other Catholic campuses in São Paulo.

The ice was broken.

Simple as the dove and shrewd as the serpent

Now it was time for apologetics.

"What's the commotion?" asked one law student of another pointing to a huddle of students around two men in the heat of a debate.

"That's Plinio and Antonio at it again. Antonio is the campus' professed Communist. He and Plinio don't see eye to eye. I'll grant you though, they can argue! And that Plinio, boy, does he have a tongue in his head!"

"Let's go see," said the other, grabbing his friend by the arm, and both joined the avid group around the two contenders.

Many years later Plinio admitted he had "used" Antonio to further the Catholic cause on campus. All he had to do was throw a few doctrinal challenges in the Communist's direction and a full-blown debate was under way. Antonio invariably attacked the Catholic Church, and it was then that Plinio waxed eloquent, as all listened. It was his way of teaching catechism.

Will you vote for me?

One day, a young man who was running for president of the Academic Center, and many years later became University Dean, approached Plinio.

"Listen, Plinio, I'm running for president of the Academic Center and have written a platform. I'd like your opinion on it."

Plinio raised an eyebrow; *hmm, we've come a long way... now he wants my opinion.*

"Gladly," he said aloud, and took it home. Next day he handed it back to the candidate.

"Here is your program. If you state in there that law students should be against the implementation of divorce in Brazil, I'll endorse it."

With this statement, Plinio was countering the campus consensus that it was "cool" and "modern" for law students to favor divorce.

Surprisingly the candidate said simply,

"Will you guarantee me the vote of the Marian Congregants?"

Suddenly Plinio realized that he and his group had become an electoral power within the campus.

Now he played hard to get.

"Well, I need to consult the other candidate and check his position not only on divorce but on other Catholic issues such as religious instruction in public schools, chaplains in the armed forces, and civil recognition of religious marriage."

In fact, the other candidate guaranteed more Catholic points and received the votes of the Marian Congregates. He was elected.

Graduation

As graduation approached, and the committee in charge of festivities made the usual preparations, Plinio made an unprecedented request. He asked that rather than having the

Plinio on the day of his graduation from the Law School of São Paulo.

traditional graduation Mass at the church of St. Francis next door, that it be celebrated in the internal courtyard of the university campus—not only a first in the century old history of the school, but also in the history of state universities in Brazil. Moreover, he asked that the Archbishop of São Paulo be invited to officiate, and Brazil's renowned Jesuit preacher, Father Leonel Franca to speak.

"If you place the invitations, the request is granted," said the university official.

"Consider it done," answered the young man nodding in acknowledgement.

On graduation day, as Plinio entered the courtyard, he was pleasantly surprised to see a beautiful altar decked with flowers. Most professors were present in ceremonial robes, some even fingering rosaries. The Archbishop had not been able to attend but sent the Vicar General in his stead, and Father Franca delivered a magnificent address.

At Communion time, Plinio stood up and approached the sacred table. Several students stood up with him, and unabashedly received the Eucharist, thus proclaiming their status as practicing Catholics.

That day Plinio received his law degree from the School of Law of the University of São Paulo.

He also received another unseen but no less real degree in Catholic Leadership from His Eucharistic Lord.

Chapter 8
Slave of Mary

"Mary adorns her clients with her merits, assists them with her power, enlightens them with her light, and kindles them with her love. She imparts her virtue to them and becomes their security, their intercessor and their all with Jesus."

—St. Louis Grignion de Montfort

On September 30, 1897 a twenty-four-year old Carmelite lay agonizing. Around her knelt the community of the Carmel of Lisieux, France. A few days before, two of her sisters in religion had asked each other what could possibly be written about her life... it had seemed so commonplace...

Now, as the astounded community watched, she suddenly opened her eyes, half raised herself in bed and fixed her ecstatic gaze on high for several seconds. Then she fell back and expired.

Devotion to Thérèse of Lisieux spread like wildfire. After Pope Pius XI canonized her in 1925, one church after another was named after her, while statues of the saint sprung up in countless shrines. Perhaps no saint single-handedly conquered the hearts of millions as easily and as speedily as the young Carmelite of Lisieux.

Plinio was no exception. After reading her autobiography, *The Story of a Soul*, he felt a keen affinity with her spirituality of the "Lit-

St. Thérèse of the Child Jesus

tle Way." Her offering of herself to God as an "expiatory victim of Love" especially moved him. The idea of self-donation to the point of heroism spoke to him deeply.

He was now twenty-two, and inwardly in need of "something more" to aid him in the progress of his spiritual life.

A novena to St. Thérèse answered in a bookshop

Ever since that day when he had cried, "Save Me, O Queen," when he had felt that Our Lady had covered him with her mantle, his spirituality had been markedly Marian.

He now recited the Rosary daily, as well as the Angelus and the Little Office of the Immaculate Conception. He was enrolled in the scapular of Our Lady of Mount Carmel, and was later to become a Carmelite tertiary. He also carried with him at all times the Miraculous Medal revealed in 1830 to Saint Catherine Labouré.

Nevertheless, he felt something was lacking. He recognized the "tugging" at his soul as divine

Plinio wearing the habit of a Third Order Carmelite.

grace knocking. He responded by saying a novena to Saint Thérèse, asking her to show him God's will in this matter of his spiritual advancement.

One day, browsing through a bookshop, Plinio's finger rested on the spine of a small volume, *Treatise on True Devotion to the Blessed Virgin Mary* by then Blessed Louis Grignion de Montfort (Pope Pius XII canonized him in 1947). The book was beautifully bound, and written in French, a double attraction for him, so he purchased it.

Apostle of Mary

In a way, Louis de Montfort and Plinio Corrêa de Oliveira had to "meet." Both their spiritualities were ardently Marian, and both had a special calling to counter the particular evil of their day.

Saint Louis de Montfort was born in Brittany, France on January 31, 1673, and died in Saint-Laurent-sur-Sévre in the Vendée on April 28, 1716 worn out by the efforts of his apostolate.

He preached tirelessly in many cities and towns, incurring the displeasure of many ecclesiastics infected with the heresy of Jansenism.

Reduced to preaching in one diocese, including the region of the Vendée, he left its people a solid legacy of faith and Marian devotion, sowing in their hearts the seeds that preserved them from the impious germ of the French Revolution. Three generations later, their faith-filled descendants valiantly took up arms against the revolutionary monster then mauling France, so that Pius XII said that "the Vendée of 1793 was the work of his [Saint Louis de Montfort's] hands."[1]

At first victorious, but eventually overwhelmed, these brave people were ruthlessly martyred for their loyalty to the monarchy and the Catholic Faith. Perhaps France owes the unexpected recovery of its Catholic Faith after the French Revolution to the blood of these and other French martyrs.

"The great incentive for his whole apostolic ministry, his great secret for attracting and giving souls to Jesus, is his devotion to Mary,"[2] affirmed again Pius XII.

Saint Louis' Slavery of Love

In his book, *True Devotion to the Blessed Virgin Mary*, Saint Louis de Montfort advocates the role of Mary as Mediatrix between Jesus Christ and men, and around her universal mediation, the French saint "built a whole Mariology that is the greatest monument of all times to the Virgin Mother of God."[3]

Statue of Saint Louis Marie Grignion de Montfort, St. Peter's Basilica, Vatican.

In *True Devotion*, Saint Louis proposes a consecration
to Mary in the terms of a "bondage or slavery of love" to
her who sacrificed her Son for each of us. In this consecration the person gives Our Lady full rights over everything
he owns whether in time or in eternity, over his life, his actions, and his merits. In one word, the person becomes the
"property" of Mary. On her part, being the most loving of
mothers and an all-powerful queen, she will do nothing but
take optimum care of her "property." Thus the saint argues
that such a consecration can only be to the advantage of
the person making it.

A parable

Every word in *True Devotion* resonated in Plinio's heart.
Still, the word "slavery" was distasteful. After all, his uncle,
the Councilor João Alfredo Corrêa de Oliveira had played
an important role in freeing the slaves in Brazil; *what was
this about "slavery to Mary" now?*

"A slave," mused Plinio, "gives up his rights and becomes the property of his owner. What possible situation
on earth could make such a condition not only legitimate
but covetable?"

As he struggled with this premise, he thought of a parable:

> "There once was a lady who had an only son. He
> was the apple of her eye, handsome, brave, kind,
> and accomplished in every way. As she was left
> a widow early in life, he was her support, solace
> and companion. This son had a friend who,
> through several guilty circumstances, came into
> serious trouble.

> One day, approaching his mother, the son pro-
> posed that the only way to deliver his friend was
> for him to place his own person in harm's way.

There was real danger in the endeavor, with the possibility of losing his life. Still, he did not want to undertake this venture without her approval. She gave her consent.

Hugging her tightly, he went on his way. Soon after, she received the news that the friend was delivered but her beloved son had been killed.

And a while later, there was a knock at her door. She opened it to find her son's friend standing before her, the picture of contrition. Though riddled with pain, she kindly invited him in. Before entering, he fell at her feet, saying: "Ma'am, I will not come into your home before you accept me as yours in place of your son. You have lost the light of your life, and are now not only a widow but alone and unprotected because of my folly. I'm your slave to do with me as you will. My life is yours, all that I own is yours, all that I am is yours. It is only right, and the least I could do."

"Yes," thought Plinio, "it would only be right."

Yes, Our Lady had also given her consent for her perfect Son to forfeit his life for the sake of our salvation, with one difference, that she had walked every step of the bloody road with him, watched him die, and then received his lifeless body in her arms.

Thinking of himself as the friend at the door, Plinio knew the Blessed Mother would have found it in her heart to raise him up, and embrace him. To him, he would be her "slave." To her, he would be a new "son." As Saint Louis de Montfort advocated, it was truly a "slavery of love."

With this difficulty resolved, Plinio could not wait to

begin the thirty-three-day preparation that Saint Louis recommends for this solemn act.

When he completed the long preparation, he wrote out the consecration on paper, as Saint Louis de Montfort recommended. Then he locked himself in his room, and lighting a candle, he consecrated himself to Our Lady as her slave of love, signing his name at the bottom. This story was told by Plinio many times to his spiritual sons. He would sometimes add, that the ceremony had been a simple one, without pomp or circumstance.

With this consecration, his devotion to Our Lady grew by leaps and bounds, communicating it to all he met. To meet Plinio was to meet Mary, and to grow in knowledge and devotion to her.

As life projected him more and more into the public eye, he was to promise Our Lady never to make a speech or deliver a talk without mentioning her name. This promise he kept to the end of his days.

Notes:

1. Pius XII, Homily for the canonization of St. Louis Marie Grignion de Montfort, *Il segreto ammirabile del Santo Rosario*, It. Tr. (Siena: Edizioni Cantagalli, 1975), pp. 7-8.

2. Ibid, p. 182.

3. Plinio Corrêa de Oliveira, Prologue to the Argentine edition of *Revolución y Contra-Revolución*, (Buenos Aires: Tradición, Familia Propriedad, 1970), p. 16.

CHAPTER 9
Public Appointment

"Nor do men light a candle and put it under a bushel,
but on a stand, and it gives light to all in the house."

—*Matt. 5:15*

"Is Father Danti in?" asked the twenty-three-year-old lawyer.

He was ushered into a traditional parlor and settled down to wait. Father José Danti was a renowned moralist with the ability of solving the most difficult problems of conscience. Plinio was struggling with one. Presently the door opened and Father Danti's handsome, intelligent face lit up at the sight of the young man he knew so well as a prominent leader in the Marian Congregation.

"Dr. Plinio! It's good to see you. Whence the pleasure?"

After the introductory pleasantries, Plinio delved into his consultation.

"Father, something has been bothering me. It's a question of conscience. But before I enter into it, I must give you some history."

"I'm all ears," said the Jesuit, crossing his legs and settling down to listen.

"Some time ago, reading the French paper, *La Croix*," began Plinio, "I learned of a movement led by General De Castelnau called Fédération Nationale Catholique. The purpose of this organization is to send political candidates a questionnaire asking them to state their position on Catholic doctrine. The organization then publishes the results

Father José Danti

as a guide to Catholic voters. I thought this a brilliant idea and with two other friends, the writer Alceu de Amoroso Lima, and the architect Heitor da Silva Costa, proposed the same idea for Brazil. Cardinal Sebastião Lemes approved it and the Catholic Electoral League is now established in Brazil."

"Wonderful, I have heard of it, a capital move," interjected Father Danti.

Then Plinio went on to quickly recap the current state of affairs. For the sake of our readers, we give a short history.

The Revolution of 1930

Indeed, Brazil was in need of an Electoral League to guide the Catholic vote. Until 1930, the nation's government was mainly in the hands of the rural aristocracy with marked conservative traits. In 1929, with the collapse of the New York Stock Exchange, Brazil's coffee market crashed, launching the country into a dramatic financial crisis. With this, a great part of the rural aristocracy lost much of its capital. Already, as cities grew industrially and commercially, the rural leaders were slowly being pushed out of the scope of influence.

At this juncture, a revolution lead by a demagogue named Getúlio Vargas deposed the conservative President Washington Luis. With the dictatorship now dubbed "New Republic" as opposed to the "Old Republic," Brazil began sliding to the left.

In 1932, São Paulo's leading classes rebelled in an attempt to re-establish the Constitutional order. As this armed movement did not have a clear ideological or Catholic substratum, Plinio did not support it, remaining uninvolved.

Though this movement failed, the initiative forced Getúlio Vargas to convoke a Constitutional Assembly to reorganize the political direction of the country.

Plinio understood the importance of the moment and conceived the idea of using the power of the Catholic movement to influence politicians, whence the formation of the Catholic Electoral League. Once formed, CEL joined the united coalition of parties of São Paulo. All of them supported the Catholic goals. Under the direction of Cardinal Leme, councils for the CEL were established in every diocese. From these councils were chosen the Catholic candidates for the Constitutional Assembly.

Appointed

Now young Plinio sat in Father Danti's parlor stunned and a little off balance. Having just graduated as a lawyer at only twenty-three, he found that Archbishop Duarte Leopoldo e Silva had nominated him one of the four Catholic candidates for São Paulo.

And here is where his conscience pricked.

"Father," Plinio continued, "I fear the Archbishop appointed me solely because I am well known in the Marian Congregation. If he personally prefers another, I would gladly step out and work for this other as if working for myself."

The shrewd, penetrating eyes of the Jesuit momentarily softened. But when he spoke his voice was firm:

"If you forgo the candidacy you will be failing in your Catholic duty. I see in you such loyalty to your Archbishop, that if your place is left vacant, another less faithful to the Hierarchy may fill it."

In other words, the good priest was saying, "by all means, pick up the gauntlet."

Thus it was with a detached and noble gesture that young Plinio stepped into public life.

Plinio at 24, the youngest delegate to the Constitutional Assembly of 1934 and the one to receive the largest number of votes ever recorded.

CHAPTER 10
Youngest Congressman

"The great transformations of history are the result of the stance that the human spirit takes in face of religion and philosophy."

—*Plinio Corrêa de Oliveira*

It was a landslide. Nominated as one of the Catholic candidates by the intrepid Archbishop Duarte, Plinio won the Congressional elections for the Federal Constitutional Assembly of 1934 with twice as many votes as the next candidate in São Paulo. This made him the youngest and most voted Congressman in all of Brazil, largely due to the Catholic vote. It was a roaring victory for Catholicism.

In an address to the Archdiocesan College, Plinio humbly characterized his election as follows:

> "Look at the European Nations after the World War. . . when wishing to immortalize the memory of so many heroes. . . they preferred to choose an anonymous soldier. . .When in 1933, twenty-four thousand Catholics in São Paulo elected me to the Constitutional Convention, they singled me out of the ranks of my brothers in the fight. The Marian youth is the spearhead of the Catholic militia. Thus it was to this organization that befell the noble task of defending Catholic Brazil in the Convention. . . Thus, to honor the blue legions of Mary, it was only right that this election go to an obscure member, who, like a new unknown soldier had no other credentials than his blue ribbon, and the burning enthusiasm of the Marian Congregants. Thus, I was chosen."[1]

This surprising victory placed Plinio in the national spotlight, projecting his influence beyond Catholic circles.

"How old is he?" asked many a Brazilian.

"Figure this, only twenty-four. . ."

"Why, a young fledgling lawyer just out of school."

There were raised eyebrows and smiles to go around.

"He will never stand up to the experienced politicians of the Constitutional Assembly."

"He will likely make a fool of himself."

On the way to Rio de Janeiro

Now, as the night train sped from São Paulo to the then Federal capital of Rio de Janeiro where the Constitutional Assembly convened, Plinio was preparing to settle down for the night when he heard a light knock on the cabin door.

"The conductor removed his hat at twenty-four-year-old me," he later related, "and asked in a respectful tone, 'are you the Congressman, sir, may I have your ticket?' "

After presenting his pass and closing the door, Plinio's thoughts played back the scene at the train station back home, a hailing crowd as he gratefully tipped his hat.

"Yes," he mused, "a new life begins. . ."

He was following in the footsteps of his ancestors, taking up the baton of leadership as had done his uncle, João Alfredo Corrêa de Oliveira, a lawyer, Prime Minister and Councilor to the Empire, and his maternal grandfather, Gabriel Ribeiro dos Santos, another lawyer and congressman. His was an old family of the rural elite, families dating back to the beginnings of Brazil, families who had built the nation.

Looking at young Plinio sitting by the window of the night express, one would have admired in him the combination of gentleman, aristocrat, and man of simple Faith, in his hand a Rosary slowly sliding through his fingers as Hail Mary after Hail Mary consecrated his public service to God.

Plinio had never compromised. Since his days as a little boy, arguing for the sacredness of the priesthood at the Théâtre des Marionettes, he had been first and foremost loyal to his Faith. On one hand his was a temperament so calm and phlegmatic that he had had to fight laziness with every ounce of energy he could muster. Fräulein Mathilde with her Germanic ways had been an invaluable asset in this aspect of his formation.

"I was so lazy," he was to confide later, "that to climb a flight of stairs was torture. To fight this lethargy, I would back up and conquer the incline in three bounds."

On the other hand, the lion in him never gave in to

Plinio during his tenure as Congressman at the Constitutional Assembly.

himself, much less to any outside influence that was not for good.

Already at twenty-two, while a student at the School of Law, he had written in the Catholic paper *O Legionário*, countering the general trend that the virtue of purity was acceptable for women but not for men,

> "...the greatly ridiculed, calumniated but sublime virtue of chastity of men who understand that only when pure, are they truly strong."[2]

Now, as he sped toward a brilliant career, he said to himself as he prayed, *"Either you are ready to give all this up at a moment's notice, as soon as your conscience demands it, or you sell out. And if you sell out, it would be better had you never been born."*[3]

Notes:

1. Plinio Corrêa de Oliveira, "Discurso como paraninfo do Colégio Arquidiocesano," Nov. 22, 1936, Revista "Echos", # 29, (1937), http://www.pliniocorreadeoliveira.info/DIS%20-%201936-11-22%20-%20Paraninfo%20Colégio%20Arquidiocesano%20de%20SP.htm.

2. Plinio Corrêa de Oliveira, "Primícias de uma geração," *O Legionário*, #90, Nov. 22, 1931, p. 2, http://www.pliniocorreadeoliveira.info/ LEG%20311122_Primícias-deumageração.htm.

3. *Memórias*, Apr. 10, 1980.

CHAPTER 11
In the Political Arena

"Fear not the swords of a thousand soldiers
ye who fight under the mantle of the Immaculate..."

—*Hymn of the Marian Congregations*

Plinio's father, Dr. João Paulo, his mother, Dona Lucilia and sister Rosée, followed him to Rio to attend the opening of the Constitutional Convention, at Tiradentes Palace. It was a solemn occasion, with the presence of civil and military authorities and the diplomatic corps.

In the midst of all the pomp and circumstance, from his place among the Congressmen Plinio's eyes searched the multitude. His mother waved. He nodded, happy to see her well seated. She smiled.

Later at the hotel, she said to him,

"My son, today you gave your mother one of the greatest joys of her life. I can still see you looking for your own and your face lighting up as you saw we were comfortable. The fact that you did this from amidst your new responsibilities in Congress meant more to me than I can say. I am still moved by this show of filial devotion."

Plinio walking the streets of Rio de Janeiro where the Constitutional Convention was held.

She knew he would be fine. A son, who at the height of

success thinks of his own, would always be, first and fore-most, her son and God's.

For Catholic Brazil

As Brazil watched, Plinio went to battle with his colleagues of the Catholic League. Their mission was to campaign in the Convention for the new Constitution to recognize certain Catholic rights that had been abolished with the establishment of the Republic in 1889. These were labeled "minimal Catholic demands." They were:

1. For the new Constitution to be implemented in God's name.
2. For the indissolubility of marriage.
3. For religious education in Public Schools, and official religious assistance to the Armed Forces.
4. For the right to vote for men and women religious.
5. For the civil recognition of religious marriage.
6. For the recognition of Sunday rest.
7. For the right of priests to fulfill the required mili-

A 125ft. statue of Christ the Redeemer stands atop the Corcovado, a mountain from which the city of Rio de Janeiro can be observed in all of its beauty.

tary service as chaplains to the Armed Forces.

Plinio campaigned tirelessly for these goals, both in personal contacts with many delegates, and on the Assembly floor where he courageously advocated and argued these points.

His was a strong, resonant voice. Even in old age, it was youthful and vigorous. He used it well on the floor during the Convention especially when debating Congressman Zoroastro Gouveia, an avowed Communist and enemy of the Catholic Church. It was a sight to behold a young man of twenty-four championing the rights of the Church and debating a bold Communist on the other side of the hall.

One officer of the Convention never forgot it. Thirty years later, Plinio was visiting Brasilia, the new capital of Brazil. As he walked through the chambers of Congress and the Senate, an old man watched him intently.

"Are you Plinio Corrêa de Oliveira?" he finally ventured.

"Yes, I am," acknowledged Plinio, and asked in turn, "Did you work for the Constitutional Assembly when I was Congressman?"

"Yes, and I'll never forget your grilling of Zoroastro Gouveia!"

The young Congressman had left a mark.

Mission accomplished

As the car pulled up to Tiradentes Palace, the Congressman stepped out. A long line of soldiers in gala uniform stood at attention. As he took his first step, they presented arms.

Plinio, always a lover of ceremony, acknowledged the salute and proceeded firmly up the walk. He was arriving for the closing of the Constitutional Convention.

Mission accomplished, he thought as he participated in

the closing ceremonies. He had been a part of an influential Catholic parliamentary committee that had obtained the approval of the "minimal Catholic demands:" the new Constitution was implemented in God's name, reestablished religious education in public schools, banned divorce, introduced civil recognition of religious marriage, and established chaplaincies in the Armed Forces and prisons.

Plinio emerged as one of the most capable and efficient leaders at the Constitutional Assembly. There were no more raised eyebrows and no more smiles.

A confession

"Dona Maria, thank you for everything," Plinio set down his suitcase in the lobby of the Hotel Regina as he extended his hand to the owner of the establishment, a pleasant, middle-aged Portuguese lady. He had lodged under her roof for nearly a year. The good lady took the offered hand and held it momentarily.

"It was a pleasure having you, Dr. Plinio, but oh, will I miss your calls to your Mamma. . ."

Plinio's eyes widened,

"Ma'am! Did you listen to them?" he asked unbelievingly. He knew he should be outraged yet felt disarmed by the simplicity and honesty of his hostess.

"I know I shouldn't have done it. . . But they were so beautiful I couldn't hang up. . ."

CHAPTER 12
Young Professor and Dutiful Son

"Because Plinio goes over and beyond the call of duty."

—*Dona Lucilia*

One of the resolutions that the new Constitution introduced was the founding of State-recognized private universities. This opened for Plinio the door to academic teaching. In 1934, the State of São Paulo appointed him Professor of History of Contemporary Civilization in the university attached to the Law School from which he had graduated only five years before.

A short while later, Plinio was appointed Professor of Modern and Contemporary History for the Colleges of "Sedes Sapientiae" and "Saint Benedict," which would later merge into the Pontifical Catholic University of São Paulo.[1]

Though only a few years older than his students, Plinio immediately won their respect by his seriousness, firmness of character and fascinating delivery.

Decades later, a lady would approach a friend of Plinio in a restaurant and with tears in her eyes recall her days as his student, "He made history come alive!"

Student strike

But the spirit of atheistic and egalitarian Communism, the scourge of the century, as foreseen by Our Lady at Fatima in 1917, was never far.

One day, as Plinio approached the university, he was warned to return home as a communist-inspired student strike was underway on campus.

"I'm teaching class," was his answer as he continued

undeterred.

No one dared stop him. He had a presence that imposed respect and a manly demeanor that discouraged nonsense. As his students saw the insurgents giving way to his progress, they fell behind him and entered the classroom. With doors shut as usual, he proceeded to deliver the day's lesson.

Suddenly the class ceased to listen and turned their attention to a distant clamor fast approaching. Soon, the striking mob was outside the locked doors, chanting and banging. Fearful eyes on the podium asked the unspoken question,

"What will you do now?"

Looking to the young man by the door, Plinio ordered, "Open the door."

The young man made his way to the door, looking back hesitatingly. "Open the door!" Plinio repeated in a commanding tone.

The young man did so, and as the clamoring mob went quiet at the sight of the respected professor standing erect at his podium, he asked in a tone of command, "What do you want?"

"Nothing, Professor," answered the mob leader suddenly subdued.

"Then close the door and let us proceed," ordered Plinio, to the young man who had first opened it.

The class continued without further incidents.

At home

Plinio always lived with his parents and, because of financial troubles, helped to support them.

In 1952 he bought a comfortable apartment on Rua Alagoas, in one of São Paulo's best areas, where the three resided until the end of their days.

The living room of Plinio's home at Rua Alagoas, where he lived for much of his life.

Plinio not only taught at the universities, but also had a law office in partnership with Paulo Ulhoa Cintra, a friend and companion in the Marian Congregation. Their principal clients were the Archdiocese of São Paulo, the Benedictine Order, and later, the Carmelite Order. Between his professional life and his work with the Catholic movement, the young Catholic leader had a full agenda, and heavy responsibilities. But at home at the dinner table with his parents (Rosée was now married) he was the attentive son, entertaining them with his daily news, and gifted conversation.

Though having some temperamental difficulties with his father, who was a devout though not militant Catholic, Plinio, nevertheless, appreciated his intelligence and many qualities, and often benefited from his shrewd counsel.

At table, Plinio broached the subjects that Dr. João Paulo,

a talented conversationalist himself, enjoyed. And his attention to Dona Lucilia, her needs, and daily concerns never waned. In turn, Dona Lucilia catered to Plinio's every preference sparing no effort to serve his favorite dishes.

"Lucilia," said a relative noticing this, "Why do you 'spoil' Plinio so?"

Her answer was characteristically maternal and to the point.

"Because Plinio goes above and beyond the call of duty."

Notes:

1. The Pontifical Catholic University of São Paulo granted Plinio a Doctorate degree based on "great and acclaimed knowledge."

CHAPTER 13
Editor of *O Legionário* and the First Idea of the TFP

"What was Legionario's ideal from the beginning? It was Catholicism, the plenitude of all true and noble ideals."

—Plinio Corrêa de Oliveira

In August 1933, Plinio was appointed Editor-in-Chief of the Catholic paper *O Legionário*, a publication of the Marian Congregation of the Parish of Saint Cecilia. Under his direction it was to become the unofficial paper of the archdiocese. Suddenly his field of influence was vast.

Under Plinio's impulse, the paper went from a biweekly to a weekly publication dealing with spiritual themes, lives of the saints, Church history, Catholic sociology, and other subjects including the fascinating column "Seven Days in Review," which kept up with both national and international events as analyzed from a Catholic viewpoint.

Between 1930 and 1940, *O Legionário* became the most important Catholic paper in Brazil, read everywhere and representing what was most dynamic in the country's youthful Catholic movement.

"Plinio's Group"

"Plinio's Group" or the *Legionário* Group was soon a household word within Catholic circles. These were the young men he had met back when he first joined the Marian Congregation. They had quickly become friends in the common ideal of fighting for a Christian Civilization, and now

Plinio standing next to the Archbishop of São Paulo, Dom Duarte Leopoldo e Silva, with a group of editors from *O Legionário*.

collaborated in the editing of *O Legionário*. Gathering around a small statue of Mary Help of Christians, and begging her to bless their endeavors, they plunged into the work of Catholic journalism. They met regularly in the basement of a house that belonged to the Marian Congregation of the Parish of St. Cecilia.

Warnings and opposition

In conformity with the teachings of Pope Pius XI, *O Legionário* informed the Catholic public of the wiles of Communism, and those of revolutionary currents lodged within rightist and extreme rightist movements.

For example, *O Legionário* wrote about the anti-Catholic persecution in Mexico between 1926–1929 which gave rise to the heroic Cristero movement. It published innumerable articles about the Spanish Civil War in which Spain fought off the Russian-backed Revolution of 1936–1939, not before giving a host of martyrs to the Church, as in Mexico. The paper was also relentless against the subtle infiltrations of Fascism and Nazism and played a vital role in defeating their influence in Brazil and South America. In twenty years, *O Legionário* published no less than 2,509 articles containing mentions and warnings against Nazism.

Looking beyond the upheaval of World War II, Plinio's clear eye also saw the looming threat of Islam in the not-so-distant future, and warned of it as well.

"The Muslim danger is immense,"[1] he wrote in 1943, and the next year, "the Muslim problem will constitute one of the gravest religious questions of our days after the war."[2] And again later that year, "The Muslim world possesses indispensable natural resources to subdue Europe. It will have at hand the necessary means to upset or paralyze, at any moment, the whole flow of the European economy."[3]

At the end of each day's work, Plinio would come home to find his mother praying by a white statue of the Sacred Heart of Jesus on a marble column.

As he turned the key in the lock, she breathed a sigh of relief, then went to meet him.

"What are you doing, Mamãe? You should be in bed," he said as he kissed and hugged her.

"Oh, just praying that you will be alright. . ."

Throughout his life, he often found Dona Lucilia keeping this maternal vigil.

Papal blessing

In 1939, Plinio and his group were greatly encouraged in

their journalistic efforts on receiving the Pontifical blessing through Cardinal Leme. Having traveled to Rome for the occasion of the election of Pope Pius XII, the newly crowned pontiff asked the Cardinal to transmit his special blessing to the group of *O Legionário*. The Cardinal did so in a letter published by *O Legionário*: ". . .the Holy Father granted his special blessing to our brave *O Legionário* and its worthy director, a true man of the Catholic press, as well as to its editors, benefactors and readers."

A chivalrous charism

From the beginning, "Plinio's Group" had a "chivalrous" character. They were known for their unwavering principles and their fighting spirit, though always accompanied by cordial and elevated manners. Though right in the 20th Century, their Catholic militancy and generosity in de-

Plinio with the Bishop of Campos, Dom Antonio de Castro Mayer, posing with a large group of members of the Marian Congregation.

fending the rights of God and His Church recalled something of the chivalry of old. This was the first nucleus of what later became the Brazilian Society for the Defense of Tradition, Family and Property—TFP.

Notes:

1. Plinio Corrêa de Oliveira, "A Questão Libanesa," *O Legionário*, # 591, Dec. 5, 1943, http://www.pliniocorreadeoliveira.info/LEG%20431205_AQUE-STÃOLIBANESA.htm.

2. Plinio Corrêa de Oliveira, "7 dias em revista," *O Legionário*, # 604, Mar. 5, 1944, http://www.pliniocorreadeoliveira.info/LEG7%20440305_Suicavaireatar-comsovieticos.htm.

3. Plinio Corrêa de Oliveira, "7 dias em revista," *O Legionário*, # 635, Oct. 8, 1944, http://www.pliniocorreadeoliveira.info/LEG7%20441008_Inteligenteeprudentepanislamismo.htm.

CHAPTER 14
The Beginnings of Progressivism

*"It would be easier to tear the Southern Cross from
the skies of Brazil than to wrench from a people faithful
to Christ, their sovereignty and Faith."*

—*Plinio Corrêa de Oliveira*

"**P**linio! Plinio! Plinio!" half a million voices chanted
as he finished his address at the Eucharistic Congress that convened in São Paulo on September 7, 1942.

In a city of then 1.5 million people, an attendance of half
a million was overwhelming proof of the resurgence of the
Faith in Brazil.

It had fallen to Plinio, as a lay Catholic leader, to address
the religious and civil authorities in a closing speech.

Plinio spoke, without a text. A famous Professor of oratory in São Paulo once said of him,

"Plinio ignores all my rules, but he is
the best orator in Brazil."

At that solemn occasion he dazzled
his audience, the multitude breaking out
in constant applause.

As he compared the assembly to
Rafael's masterpiece, "Triumph of the
Eucharist," he electrified the crowd by
his loving eloquence on the soul and
temperament of the Brazilian people,
and spoke of Brazil's vocation as a

Plinio delivering one of his many speeches to
Brazil's Catholic movement.

Catholic nation.

In masterful words, he painted for them the beauty, both spiritual and material, of this nation they were called to lead, and the grandeur awaiting that same nation if it were faithful to God and Rome:

> "This message echoes the divine precept, 'Give to Caesar what is Caesar's and to God what is God's.' The applause of this multitude confirms principles that the challenges of time were unable to erase... Brazil was given the providential mission of growing within its own frontiers, in developing here the splendors of a genuinely Roman Catholic and Apostolic civilization... It would be easier to tear the Southern Cross[1] from the skies of Brazil than to wrench from a people faithful to Christ, their sovereignty and Faith...
>
> "Leaders of our nation, Give to God what is God's and to Caesar what is Caesar's. Explore the riches of our soil; pattern our civil institutions after the maxims of the Church, which are the essence of Christian Civilization. Support the Holy Church of God in all you can, so it may shape the national soul according to grace... Make Brazil a prosperous, organized and dynamic nation, and the Church will make Brazilians a great people...."[2]

The virus of Progressivism

It was a beautiful time for the Faith in Brazil. Again, the country was reaping the effects of the heroic efforts of Pope Saint Pius X against Modernism, which he called, "the synthesis of all heresies."[3] The Church enjoyed complete peace in a climate of total trust and cohesion among the faithful, the religious orders and the Sacred Hierarchy.

This climate of religious fervor was also true in other countries of South America.

Little did Brazil suspect that a mutant form of the virus of Modernism, later labeled "Progressivism," had landed on its shores. It came in the form of European movements, excellent in themselves but infected with strains of this virus. This was mainly a tendency (sometimes a true obsession) to dilute Catholic dogma and morals to "fit in" with the neo-pagan world.

Though the mass of Catholic public opinion was sound, elements within the Liturgical Movement[4] and Catholic Action[5] began to adhere to this new mentality. As President of the Archdiocesan Board of Catholic Action, Plinio was on hand to detect the first manifestations of this influence.

First signs of "Progressivism"

The first sign of that "updated" mentality was disdain for traditional Catholic devotions such as the Sacred Heart of Jesus, Our Lady, the saints, holy images, the rosary, and the Way of the Cross. These "passé" practices were to be replaced with an official "community prayer."

Traditional schools of spirituality such as those of Saint Ignatius Loyola and his Spiritual Exercises, and Saint Alphonsus Liguori were also discouraged.

Then, certain norms of the classic moral code as the avoidance of near occasions of sin and the combat of disorderly passions were made to look as "no longer applying." For example, under the pretext of taking "Christ to others," people were encouraged to frequent morally dangerous places such as shady nightclubs; a practice formerly opposed by Catholic moralists.

On the other hand, a type of "class struggle" between the clergy and the laity was introduced undermining the hierarchical and monarchical character of the Church. "The reformers tended to eliminate the basic difference between the sacramental priesthood of the priests and the common priesthood of the laity, suggesting an egalitarian and democratic view of the Church."[6]

Quoting the Communist theoretician, Antonio Gramsci, Plinio alluded to this situation,

> "From outside the Catholic citadel, with intentions radically opposite to mine, the Communist theoretician Antonio Gramsci nevertheless saw the same reality I saw when he said, 'Democratic Catholicism can do what socialism cannot: it can rally, organize, energize, and then commit suicide.'"[7]

Plinio, whose special charisma was that of gatekeeper, saw the infectious malady and saw it clearly. Before the brewing storm, he decided someone had to assume the tragic role of lightning rod. As the new mentality made more and more inroads into the ranks of the faithful, he decided to do what he did best—sound the alarm.

Notes:

1. The constellation over Brazil, called the "Southern Cross."

2. Plinio Corrêa de Oliveira, "Saudação às autoridades civis e militares," *O Legionário*, Sept. 7, 1942, http://www.pliniocorreadeoliveira.info/DIS%20-%201942-09-07%20-%20IV%20Congresso%20Eucaristico.htm.

3. Pope St. Pius X, Encyclical *Pascendi Dominici Gregis,* Sept. 8, 1907, no. 39, in Claudia Carlen, I.H.M., *The Papal Encyclicals 1903-1939,* (n.c.: McGrath Publishing Company, 1981), p. 89, http://www.vatican.va/holy_father/pius_x/encyclicals/documents/hf_p-x_enc_19070908_pascendi-dominici-gregis_en.html.

4. In Brazil, the Liturgical Movement began in 1933 with a Benedictine Monk from Germany, Dom Martin Michler. Cf. Roberto de Mattei, *The Crusader of the 20th Century*, p. 75.

5. In Brazil, Catholic Action was founded in 1935. It tried to coordinate all the Catholic associations and works already in existence in the country, subordinating them to the same guidelines. Cf. Ibid., pp. 75-76.

6. Ibid., p. 74.

7. *Um Homem, Uma Obra, Uma Gesta,* Entrevistando Plinio Corrêa de Oliveira, p. 55.

CHAPTER 15
A Bombshell Book

"Let us therefore lie in wait for the just, because he is contrary to our doings, and upbraideth us with transgressions of the law, and divulgeth against us the sins of our way of life."

—*Wisdom 2:12*

As Plinio worked alone in the basement, he fought for concentration as the sounds of music and youthful laughter trickled down from upstairs. Up until that time in Catholic Brazil, young men and women met separately for parties, each with their own club or confraternity. Otherwise, girls and boys met at church socials, open functions or family parties. But the new "wave" had introduced gatherings of un-chaperoned young men and women in Catholic circles, and there was the obvious "flirtatious" tone in the air.

Plinio leaned back in his chair, his eyes on the ceiling, *this is one more seed of an unparalleled sexual revolution. . . if we don't stop this train, it will lead to free-love, and who-knows what else. . .* The young leader smiled wryly as he imagined the explosive reaction around him if he were to air this piece of Plinian prognostic. He could hear it, "For goodness sake, Plinio, why do you always exaggerate! The kids are only having innocent fun! Don't be so old-fashioned-stuffy!"

He raised a quizzical eyebrow, shrugged a shoulder and returned to work.

Presently the door opened and a young man stepped in, a broad smile on his face,

"Plinio, drop the work! Join the fun!"

"Thanks, friend, but I have a lot of things to go over for

the next publication of *O Legionário*," answered Plinio in his usual kind demeanor.

Suddenly the smile was gone from the face of the young visitor.

"Plinio, you are just too serious. Lighten up! There are winds of change, you know. Either you join up with the new [progressivist] mentality or you will be left behind, because this mentality is advancing on all fronts. There are great plans for it."

These words of a future important politician rang like a threat. But Plinio Corrêa de Oliveira was not a man to be intimidated.

He felt the time had come for him to do something about that liberalizing trend within Catholic Action. Delving into pontifical documents, he wrote a book.

Published in 1943 with the title, *In Defense of Catholic Action*, the book clearly showed that the changes being proposed within the Catholic movement were contrary to Catholic doctrine.

The Apostolic Nuncio to Brazil and future Cardinal, Archbishop Bento Aloisio Masella wrote the book's preface, while the Imprimatur came from Monsignor Antonio de Castro Mayer, at the direction of the new Archbishop of São Paulo, Dom José Gaspar de Affonseca e Silva.

Plinio hoped that even if the book did not restrain the nefarious mentality invading the Catholic world, it would at least confine it to a small area. He knew that those who had already disposed their souls to its sway would adhere to it no matter what.

In any case, he knew the risk: either the book would deal a mortal blow to Progressivism, or it could give rise to much incomprehension and ill-feelings toward the "*Le-*

gionário Group," crippling its influence.

Kamikaze

It was a bombshell.

Though Plinio kept the book strictly on a doctrinal level, refraining from pointing fingers, it deeply rocked Catholic public opinion.

Many of the errors later pointed out in 1985 by then Cardinal Ratzinger in his book, *The Ratzinger Report*, were denounced in the pages of *In Defense of Catholic Action*.

Some liked it. Many did not. Those who liked it were enthusiastic. Those who did not were furious.

The author received many letters of support, including twenty from the Episcopate and one from the Provincial of the Company of Jesus for Central Brazil, Father L. Riou, famed for his piety.

On the other hand, others clamored,

"The Church will condemn this book!"

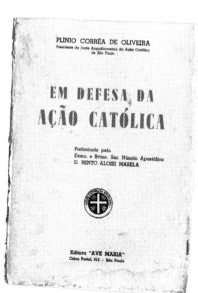

Cover of the book, *In Defense of Catholic Action*, published in 1943. The book denounced a series of errors and modernist ideas then infiltrating the Catholic movement.

One bishop was so incensed after reading it that he declared it deserved to be burned in public.

"How can a bishop wish to burn a book prefaced by the Pope's representative?" mused Plinio with his friends.

After the first cloud of dust settled, Progressivism was compared to "a lion that though still alive and dangerous only had three paws,"[1]

Still, the book so rocked Catholic opinion around the "*Legionário* Group" that Plinio wrote:

> "It was a kamikaze operation. It would either blow progressivism out of the water or it would blow us up. It blew us up. Within Catholic circles some applauded; others were furious; and the great majority felt deeply estranged."[2]

A storm of calumnies

And then the storm broke. Unmasked, many in the progressivist faction launched a barrage of calumnies and slanders against the "*Legionário* Group." All accusations were vague and without base or proof.

The new Archbishop of São Paulo, Dom Carlos Carmelo Vasconcelos Motta, a man whose disposition was as imperious as it was contrary to the views of *O Legionário* lost no time in trimming the wings of the publishing team. As a consequence, Plinio Corrêa de Oliveira lost his position as President of Catholic Action and director of *O Legionário*.

Unable to sustain the violence of the storm, many of Plinio's friends went their own way. Plinio was left with only eight faithful companions. In a short time, he went from acclaimed Catholic leader to one of the most controversial personalities in the Catholic world.

At the same time, in his law-practice, Plinio lost his main clients, the Archdiocese and the Benedictines, eventually losing the Carmelites as well.

The dark night of a heavy ostracism descended upon Plinio and his group. There was nothing left to do but to stay together, pray and hope.

Notes:
1. Eloi Magalhães Taveiro, "Para evitar as prescrições da Historia," *Catolicismo*, # 270, June 1973.
2. Plinio Corrêa de Oliveira, "Kamikaze," *Fôlha de São Paulo*, Feb. 15, 1969, http://www.pliniocorreadeoliveira.info/FSP%2069-02-15%20Kamikaze.htm.

CHAPTER 16
In the "Catacombs"

"We shall live to fight again, and to strike another blow."

—*Lord Alfred Tennyson*

In February of 1945 the small group had rented a place, three rooms and a kitchen, at 665 Martim Francisco Street. Here, around Plinio's small statue of Our Lady Help of Christians, the group met every night without fail.

"Our center needs a paint job," suggested one of Plinio's friends.

"Good idea," he answered.

Armed with paint and brushes, they were busy at work.

The truth was, Plinio had to find something to keep his group active while weathering the storm brought on by his book.

They were that isolated. It felt like a real "catacomb."

Years later Plinio recalled,

> "Oblivion overwhelmed us when we were still in the flower of youth. This was the sacrifice which was foreseen and accepted. . . .

> "With the book though, budding progressivism suffered a blow from which it has not yet recovered."[1]

But Plinio was a true leader, giving his best at such hours. His first cousin and faithful follower, Dr. Adolpho Lindenberg, describes him for us:

> "Only those who lived with Plinio in his early years of adulthood were able to know his vitality, good humor and personal radiance. It was something

powerful! Age, heartbreaks, disappointments, ill-
nesses and a horrific car crash added a veil of suffering. . . . But I knew him at his apex, with his
imposing figure, his certainties about the things he
would say, and his ceremonious and affable way of
dealing with people. He was a leader to the full extent of the word."[2]

Soon, the small first-floor apartment was transformed.
Besides all his other gifts, Plinio had a keen sense of order
and aesthetics. He believed in the power of "ambiance" to

Plinio with a few faithful followers at Martim Francisco Street.

influence man's tendencies for better or for worse. Thus, he sustained that a room elegantly, yet warmly furnished can call a man to live up to his own dignity, higher aspirations, and encourage lofty conversations. Other cold, impersonal or vulgar ambiances can do just the opposite.

With contributions of furniture, books and pictures from the several members and himself, the rooms were furnished and decorated with taste so as to feel like a fitting first headquarters of the old "*Legionário* Group" now in transition. For despite apparent defeat, Plinio never ceased to believe in his calling, and continued encouraging his friends,

"One day our group will grow and spread across the globe," he asserted. His confidence inspired the others.

Prayer, study and conviviality

Meanwhile, they prayed, studied, and shared many a conversation. Plinio was as fascinating a conversationalist as an orator. His ease in both sprang from his desire to communicate. Expansive, naturally and respectfully friendly, with a shimmering intelligence, a keen psychological insight, and humility to match, he engaged both prince and pauper and all in between with the same grace and ease adapted to the status and capacity of each.

Observing a homeless man begging outside of church one day, he later commented in a meeting, "*this is one of the notions in which the contemporary man is poorest. He does not know how to comprehend the beauty of a soul, he does not know how to understand how beautiful any soul is, the soul of the last ragamuffin which we find drunk in the street.*"[3]

He loved souls as he saw them bathed in the blood of Our Lord Jesus Christ, and treated each as a potential heir to Heaven.

Loyal friend

If he so loved the soul of a homeless man, much more did he love the souls of those who had stood by him through thick and thin. In all of his life he was never to forget their courage and loyalty. No one knew the meaning of "friend" better than Plinio.

Manly, without sentimental affectation, yet full of true, lofty sentiment, he kept his group so cohesive and hopeful that they became a true family of souls.

He also knew the importance of the spiritual life and reception of the Sacraments and encouraged Mass attendance and Communion, or at least Communion every day. (At that time, it was an accepted practice for priests to distribute Communion outside of Mass. Though the rule of the Church has not changed, custom has.)

"Gentlemen, it's five to midnight," he often warned at the Fazano Coffee Shop, a favorite meeting place. At this, coffee cups came down and forks were laid to rest. At that time, the Eucharistic fast began at midnight, and Plinio and his group were daily communicants.

Devotion to Mary and the Rosary

Their piety was rooted in devotion to Mary. For Plinio, Mother and Divine Son were inseparable. Thus he prayed,

> "Oh my Mother, at the moment that I receive the Holy Eucharist, I ask Jesus the Host through Thy intercession to give me an ardent devotion to Thee so as to unite myself with Him."[4]

He loved to think of Mary Most Holy hastening the coming of the Messiah with her prayers.

> "Isn't it true that Our Lord comes to us in Holy Communion? Isn't it true that we can and should

ask her, when we prepare ourselves to receive Him, for some of the thoughts that she had when she received Our Lord in the Incarnation?"[5]

And, "When we receive this same Jesus Christ in Holy Communion, do we ask ourselves how He finds our hospitality? Do we at least offer the simple luxury of a clean house when He condescends to come down to our hut?"[6]

They also recited the full Rosary every day. Plinio had a great devotion to the Holy Rosary and once said, "To hold a Rosary in your hand is like holding in your hand a corner of Our Lady's mantle."

The "Chinese River"

"Our suffering on that occasion," wrote Plinio later, *"was like getting scalped. In that period we started to accept misfortune as it came and resign ourselves with what Providence had allowed. And we began to re-equip ourvelves so as to lead, in the catacombs, a life as bearable as we could. . . . I believe that was the most beautiful time of our lives. . . a time of tremendous trial but also one of perseverance."*[8]

During this period, Plinio often referred to the life of Job in the Old Testament. He read and meditated on that so many times that the pages of the Book of Job in his Bible turned yellow, and the edges became worn.

Plinio often referred to those "catacomb" years as their "Chinese River." He derived the expression from an old Geography class back at Colégio São Luis in which the teacher taught that some Chinese rivers frequently and dramatically changed courses through history, sometimes giving the impression they are ready to flow into the sea, and then turning sharply inland again.

"With us there was one difference," said Plinio, "Our

Chinese River knocked us for a loop, because not only did it change course left and right, but suddenly plunged into the earth."[9]

Subterranean rivers are a geographical fact. In the "catacomb" years, they felt buried. Yet, their ideals took shape from much study, conversation and prayer. It was as if they were doing a long "vigil of arms" from which they would issue forth ready for new combats.

"So much so, that when the river began to emerge from the earth, we had all of our goals, doctrinal positions, internal organization and spirit delineated. Now, it was only a matter of growing [in number]"[10] said Plinio years later.

Notes:

1. Plinio Corrêa de Oliveira, "Kamikaze," in *Folha de S. Paulo*, Feb. 15, 1969.

2. Adolpho Lindenberg, "Plinio Corrêa de Oliveira: mentalidade, gostos, trato, conversa, relacionamento social," in *Plinio Corrêa de Oliveira, Dez Anos Depois*, (São Paulo: Associação dos Fundadores da TFP—Tradição Família Propriedade, 2005). p. 52.

3. Plinio Corrêa de Oliveira, "Thirst for Souls," *Circulares aos propagandistas de "Catolicismo," aos sócios e militantes da TFP*, (mimeographed), Vol. 7, p. 5.

4. Plinio Corrêa de Oliveira, "The Epic Spirit," *Circulares* , Vol. 3, p. 8.

5. Plinio Corrêa de Oliveira, " Commentaries on The Treatise of True Devotion," *Circulares*, Vol. 7, p. 2.

6. Ibid.

7. Lecture, Jun. 3, 1981.

8. Fr. David Francisquini, "A sombra da Cruz na vida e na obra de Plinio Corrêa de Oliveira," in *Plinio Corrêa de Oliveira, Dez Anos Depois*, p. 159.

9. Lecture Jul. 7, 1973.

10. Lecture Jul. 7, 1973.

*"The only title I ever wanted was
that of Roman Catholic."*

—*Plinio Corrêa de Oliveira*

"**G**entlemen, a letter from Rome!" Plinio smiled broadly, waiving a white envelope, as he hung his hat on a peg.

It had come by the morning post. Never was there a more welcome sight than the emblem of the Holy See.

During six years of ostracism, nothing hurt more than Rome's silence, which hung heavy on their Catholic hearts. Plinio and his Group had gone out on a limb risking all in defense of the Church, yet the Church said nothing.

Not only had the lay members of the small group been ostracized, but the two priests who had given them ample support and were considered a part of the old "*Legionário* Group," Fathers Antonio de Castro Mayer, and Geraldo de Proença Sigaud[1] were both removed from their parishes and positions. Father Castro Mayer lost his position as Vicar General and seminary professor, and Father Sigaud his youth ministry. Both were moved to distant posts.

But Pius XII was not asleep. He was merely studying the case of this young Brazilian group with all the care and deliberation for which the Vatican is famed.

The previous year the Pope suddenly nominated Father Sigaud as Bishop of Jacarezinho. And then Father Mayer, who had given *In Defense of Catholic Action* its Imprimatur, was made Bishop of Campos. These two nominations shocked Catholic circles. They were clear indications that the Holy Father sided with those who had championed the book.

And now, Plinio read the contents of this morning's letter to his eager friends:

> Vatican Palace,
> February 26, 1949
>
> Illustrious Sir,
> Moved by your filial dedication and piety, you offered the Holy Father the book *In Defense of Catholic Action*, in which you reveal extreme care and diligence.
> His Holiness rejoices with you for having explained and defended Catholic Action, which you know in its entirety and hold in high esteem, with penetration and clarity, so that it has become clear to everyone how opportune it is to study and promote this auxiliary form of the hierarchical apostolate.
> The August Pontiff, with all his heart, presents his wishes that this work may bear rich and seasoned fruits, and that you may reap from it many and great consolations. And as a token that this shall come to pass, he grants you the Apostolic Blessing.
> For my part, with due consideration, I remain devotedly yours,
>
> G. B. Montini [Later Paul VI]
> Substitute Secretary of State [2]

Fazano's served plenty of coffee and pastries that evening, and the next morning there was a special thanksgiving in each of their hearts at Holy Communion. Who cared if the whole world was against you, if

Rome was for you?

Pius XII had spoken, and now the ice built around Plinio and his group could melt.

But it did not.

Despite the Pope's clear opinion, progressivist circles persisted in the campaign of ostracism by employing the unyielding tactic of a heavy silence around all that concerned Plinio and companions.

Fatima

Shortly before this time Plinio had become more deeply acquainted with the message of Our Lady of Fatima to three little Portuguese shepherds in 1917. These apparitions were to play a vital role in his life. For him, Fatima confirmed and explained everything he had so far detected. Now, as World War II raged, Plinio was a living, attentive witness of the truth of Our Lady's prophetic words:

The Basilica of Our Lady of Fatima stands a short distance from the spot where Our Lady appeared to Lucia, Francisco and Jacinta in 1917.

"If they do what I shall tell you, many souls will be saved, and there will be peace. The war is going to end [WWI], but if they do not stop offending God, another even worse war will begin in the reign of Pius XI. Behold, a night illuminated by an unknown light will be the great sign that God shall give you that He is going to punish the world for its crimes by means of war, hunger, and persecutions of the Church and of the Holy Father." [3]

He was just as attentive to her other prophecy about atheistic and egalitarian Communism:

". . .[Russia] will spread its errors throughout the world, promoting wars and persecutions of the Church. The good will be martyred; the Holy Father will have much to suffer, and several nations will be annihilated." [4]

Plinio had already seen the first attempts of the Communist ideology in his country, with the revolution of 1930. He also knew that the undermining of Catholicism in Brazil could only profit this subversive ideology.

The years passed but the devotion to Fatima remained. So far, the Communists had been semi-masked in Brazil. Soon, Plinio would have to offer open battle to the unmasked Red danger. He always did it under the banner of Fatima.

Notes:

1. Many years later, both bishops went their separate ways and were no longer affiliated with Plinio's group. Bishop Mayer joined Archbishop Lefebvre's movement.

2. Plinio Corrêa de Oliveira, *In Defense of Catholic Action*, (Spring Grove, Penn.: The American Society for the Defense of Tradition, Family, Property—TFP, 2006), p. 1.

3. Antonio A. Borelli and John R. Spann, *Our Lady of Fatima, Prophecies of Tragedy or Hope?* (Pleasantville, N.Y.: The American Society for the Defense of Tradition, Family, and Property, 1986), 2nd. ed., p. 51.

4. Ibid., pp. 51-52.

CHAPTER 18
Expansion

"Vision is the art of seeing things invisible."

—*Jonathan Swift*

"Dr. Plinio, will you take care of my boys?" Father Walter Mariaux's genial face was slightly clouded yet confident, as he lowered his broad Germanic frame into a comfortable chair.

Walter Mariaux was an impressive Jesuit. Tall, broad, determined and brilliant, he had one of those personalities that hushed conversations when he stepped into a room. Plinio describes him best:

> "Blond, very tall, Herculean, exuberant health, ample gestures, the hands of a field marshal, he always gives a first impression of one who is robust and determined. . . I have never known a richer personality in contrasting elements that were, nonetheless, harmonious."[1]

An active anti-Nazi, Fr. Mariaux had been forced to leave Germany, and after serving in Rome as World Director of the Marian Congregations, had landed in Brazil while the war still raged.

One of his first wishes was to meet Plinio, whose articles in *O Legionário* he avidly read back in Rome. They became fast friends.

Settling in São Paulo, Father Mariaux dedicated his time and energy to the Marian Congregation at the Colégio São Luis, which, under his impulse grew numerous and robust.

In 1949, the stalwart priest was recalled to Rome. At this juncture, ten of the young men formerly under his direc-

Father Walter Mariaux and a group of young men directed by him.

tion knocked on the door of 665 Martim Francisco, and asked Plinio to take them into his group. Later, others came. Among these was a young man who followed the call to the priesthood. He was José Luiz MarinhoVillac, later Canon, and now Monsignor Villac, a brave and loyal friend to whom Plinio's group owes much to this day.

Now, one center was no longer enough, and a second apartment was rented followed by a third in 1952 where an "auditorium" was installed.

Catolicismo

In January of 1951, Bishop Antonio de Castro Mayer founded the cultural monthly *Catolicismo* (*Catholicism*) in Campos. The paper was edited in São Paulo by Dr. José Carlos Castilho de Andrade, one of Plinio's first friends, and assembled by a staff of members of Plinio's group. Plinio himself was one of its main contributors and inspirers.

Like *O Legionário* of old, *Catolicismo* dealt with a wide range of subjects of interest to the Catholic mind, also analyzing events in light of Catholic doctrine.

Introducing the importance of "tendencies"

One of the most popular columns was Plinio's "Ambiances, Customs and Civilizations" which many a reader confessed to reading before all other articles.

In ACC, Plinio analyzed photos depicting traditional ambiances, from palaces to pubs; customs, from fashions to folklore; civilizations, from art to academics.

He then juxtaposed these pictures to modern-day photos of the

First edition of the monthly *Catolicismo*, published by Plinio and his group.

same. Often comparing a wide range of Christian traditions to today's lack of them, he made the case for what he termed the "Revolution in the Tendencies."

"The most powerful driving force of the Revolution is in the disordered tendencies,"[2] he writes in Revolution and Counter-Revolution, sustaining that a systematic undermining of our ambiances, customs, and civilizations—in one word, our culture—leads to the erosion of our way of thinking, and, consequently, of our beliefs. By using culture to influence our tendencies, this process slowly changes our ideas.

Plinio believed that "culture" has a lot to do with a solid faith and Christian principles or the lack of them. He became a "specialist" in this field of the manipulation of man's tendencies, often giving whole seminars on the subject.

Thus, for example, many parents today would like to

raise chaste daughters to be virgins on their wedding day. Many teach them God's law and nature's principles in this regard, yet the culture undercuts that very law and those very principles every step of the way.

Fashions undermine modesty, customs expose girls to every un-chaperoned danger, voyeurism launches them early in the public eye, rock and roll "liberates" their movements, movies with covert or overt sexual content excite their imaginations—at this point, what can a parent possibly say to make a difference when their "tendencies" have been saturated with the opposite message?

Again, how futile is preaching respect for elders and a sense of family unity, when fast food is the word of the day, when the father no longer sits daily at the head of an inviting dinner table, with the mother on his right and the children gathered around? When TV reigns supreme in almost every room of the house promoting selfish individualism, spewing violence, and lawlessness? Again, what can a parent possibly say to counter the wrong message?

Architecture also sends "tendential" messages. Perhaps the most glaring example is that of churches that look like auditoriums, and which have become just that—gathering places where all talk, laugh and "catch up" hardly aware that in an out-of-the-way corner is the Holy of Holies, the Living God under the Eucharistic Species.

In Ambiances, Customs and Civilizations, Plinio strove to show the stark contrast between Christian Civilization—a fosterer of virtues–and advancing Neo-Pagan Culture—a fosterer of rebellion.

He thus disclosed to the public that "missing ingredient" that many a family, struggling to rear God-fearing children, often misses: the leaven of wholesome customs involving fashions, art, music, manners and all those more "subliminal" aspects of life that, nevertheless, support our "tendencies" and not just our minds along the path of truth. Plinio often quoted Paul Bourget, *"One must live as one thinks, under pain of sooner or later ending up thinking as one lives."*[3]

In time, *Catolicismo* became widely read in Brazil, becoming a true pole of thought.

A means to new contacts

Catolicismo was like a ship built from the wreckage of *O Legionário* whose hull now opened a new era and a new scope of influence. The result was many new contacts, interested in the ideals of Plinio and his group, which now was called the "*Catolicismo* Group."

Uniting their efforts, the members of *Catolicismo* launched a true work of expansion of their new paper. They traveled, visited friends, and organized talks around the country and abroad.

Soon, beginning with Rio, groups of friends and collaborators were established in several other Brazilian cities.

Two illustrious members

"Sir, you were over the speed limit, may I see your license," said the policeman.

As the driver presented his ID, the officer suddenly dropped to one knee.

"Oh Sir, I'm sorry. Can I have your blessing?"

The driver smiled, wished him well and went on.

Later that day, a flustered policeman said to his wife,

"You won't believe what I did! I almost fined Prince Pedro Henrique de Orleans Bragança!"

Though the monarchy in Brazil was long gone, nostalgic

echoes of its beneficent rule still lingered in Brazilian hearts.

A short history

Prince Pedro Henrique was the great-grandson of the last Emperor of Brazil, Pedro II, father of Dona Isabel, the benevolent princess who freed the slaves in 1888.

Princess Isabel was married to the Count D'Eu of the ancient house of Orleans, a branch of the Capetian royal family, the oldest in Europe. Their first son, Prince Pedro Gastão, renounced the throne, passing the succession to Prince Luiz known as "The Perfect Prince." He was born in Brazil in 1878, and exiled in 1889 along with the Imperial Family by the incoming Republic. In 1908, Prince Luiz married Princess Maria Pia of Bourbon-Two Sicilies. During the First World War he fought on the side of England and died of his wounds in 1920.

Prince Luiz longed to return to Brazil and attempted to do so in 1906. As his ship approached Rio, he wrote in his diary,

> "I am about to see Rio once again. . . For seventeen years now I have dreamed of this moment. . . How many times in my dreams I have visited its shores. . . I run to the places of my childhood. . . but then cruel destiny distances and hides them from me and I find myself once again in mid-ocean unable to assuage my longing. . . Will the same happen today?"[4]

Unfortunately, the government denied him entry and he had no remedy but to return to Europe.

In 1920, the year he died, the Brazilian Government lifted the banishment imposed on the Imperial Family.

In 1945, Prince Luiz's son, Prince Pedro Henrique, born in 1909, and heir "by right" returned to Brazil with his wife, Princess Maria Elizabeth of Wittelsbach, granddaughter of the last king of Bavaria, Louis III, and their family.

Though back in Brazil, they faced destitution as the Republic had confiscated all property belonging to the Imperial Family. Compassionate friends donated a house, which Prince Pedro Henrique sold and bought a small ranch in the south of Brazil where he dedicated himself to farming. He later moved back to Rio.

Prince Pedro Henrique and Princess Maria Elizabeth had twelve children. Though facing a life with reduced means, they were exemplary parents, and their children have fond memories of life on the farm. The pious Princess would often tell her children not to worry about their future, "for God never abandons large families."[5]

The Prince and Plinio

Back in Paris in 1912, Dona Lucilia and her mother, Dona Gabriela, were attending Holy Mass at the Church of St. Germain l'Auxerrois one day, when they noticed a distinguished lady, who, every so often, stole a discreet look at them.

"Princess Isabel," whispered Dona Gabriela in her daughter's ear.

"Yes, Mother, I recognized her too," whispered back Dona Lucilia.

To the Princess, in turn, the two distinguished ladies seemed compatriots, and at the end of Mass, she had her lady-in-waiting approach them with an invitation to meet her in the sacristy. The Princess graciously invited the Ribeiro dos Santos-Corrêa de Oliveira family to a tea in her residence at Boulogne-sur-Seine on the outskirts of Paris.

At this typically Brazilian tea, five-year-old Plinio and four-year-old Prince Pedro Henrique met and played together.

When Prince Pedro Henrique was thirteen years old, he traveled with his family on a visit to Brazil. On this occasion, Dona Gabriela invited them for a lunch at her house, and there the Prince and Plinio, now thirteen and fourteen, renewed their friendship, which only grew through the years.

Between them there was always a great ideological affinity. Prince Pedro Henrique's mother, Princess Maria Pia of Bourbon-Two Sicilies, was profoundly Catholic, of a Faith tried and forged by her family's battle at the side of Blessed Pius IX against the liberal, revolutionary currents that subverted Italy in the 19th century. This revolution ultimately led to the usurpation of the Neapolitan Throne and the Papal States.

In 1945, when Prince Pedro Henrique and his family returned to Brazil to stay, Plinio traveled to Rio to greet the Prince. Plinio was then already a notable Catholic leader and though a monarchist by persuasion, he did not participate in any monarchist organization, deeming this stance more beneficial to the Catholic cause as monarchist propaganda, at that time, was still illegal.

In turn, every time Prince Pedro Henrique traveled to São Paulo, he attended the meetings of "Plinio's Group."

Having raised his children in the love of their Faith, and consecrated each one to Our Lady from infancy, Prince Pedro Henrique wished those of his sons that felt disposed to Plinio's "school of thought" to benefit from this solid Catholic formation.

Prince Pedro Henrique's heir, Prince Luiz and his third son and second heir[6], Prince Bertrand, showed signs of a fervent interest in that direction, as Prince Luiz attests,

> "My brother Dom Bertrand and I were particularly avid for that good influence because of a series of

factors, including primarily the God-given graces received through the intercession of Our Blessed Mother, to Whom our parents consecrated us from birth (we wore only blue and white clothes to honor the Mother of God until we turned three).

"The Catechism classes mother gave us ever since we began to acquire the use of reason also made a profound impression on our souls...

"Added to the influence of the Catechism taught by my mother was the influence of my paternal grandmother who was herself very much given to an ultramontane[7] type of religiosity. The union between Altar and Throne was vividly present in her way of being, thinking, and in the stories she would tell about our family. Then we also read books on the Middle Ages, Charlemagne, St. Louis IX King of France, and chivalry. We were enchanted with people's consistent way of feeling and thinking throughout a whole historical era

Prince Luiz de Orleans e Bragança, heir to the throne of Brazil, with Plinio on his left, and his brother Prince Bertrand on his right.

oriented by the teachings of the Church. All that marked our souls profoundly."[8]

So it was that Prince Pedro Henrique gave one more proof of his esteem for Plinio by entrusting him and his group with the continuing formation of his sons, Prince Luiz and Prince Bertrand. Both brothers were already members of the Marian Congregation in the early 1950's, being outstanding in their piety and abnegation.

Their dedicated membership in the "*Catolicismo* Group," and later in the Brazilian TFP, was and is an exalted honor to this day.

Notes

1. Plinio Corrêa de Oliveira, "Em Itaicí," *O Legionário*, # 609, Apr. 9, 1944.

2. Plinio Corrêa de Oliveira, *Revolution and Counter-Revolution*, (York, PA: The American Society for the Defense of Tradition, Family, and Property, 1993), p. 29.

3. P. Bourget, *Le démon du midi*, Librarie Plon , Paris 1914, vol.II, p. 375.

4. Prince Luiz de Orleans e Bragança, *Sob o Cruzeiro do Sul*, (Impressora Montreux, 1913), apud Alcindo Gonçalves, "1903 *A Tribuna* redige *habeas corpus* em favor da família imperial brasileira," http://www.novomilenio.inf.br/santos /h0297.htm.

5. Prince Bertrand de Orleans e Bragança, Closing Talk at 2006 TFP Summer Camp in Louisiana.

6. Prince Eudes, second son of Prince Pedro Henrique renounced the succession.

7. "Ultramontane" meaning "Beyond the Mountains" was the name given to the French who resisted the atheistic and anti-monarchical French Revolution and its anti-Papal, Gallican bent. The term "Ultramontane" has become synonymous with Catholic counter-revolutionary action.

8. Prince Luiz de Orleans e Bragança, "Plinio Corrêa de Oliveira e a Família Imperial do Brasil," in *Dez Anos Depois*, p. 40.

CHAPTER 19

Revolution and Counter-Revolution—a "Prophetic" Book

"A theology and philosophy of history are born above all during periods of crisis in the history of man."[1]

—Cardinal J. Ratzinger, (Pope Benedict XVI)

History is fascinating when seen from the perspective of a battle between good and evil begun in heaven with Saint Michael's battle cry of, "Who is like onto God!" and Lucifer's rebellion, and on earth between God's command and the disobedience of our first parents. As Saint Ignatius Loyola aptly puts it, it is a battle between "Our Lord and Lucifer as two captains armed one against the other, and calling all men to their banners."

Similarly, St. Augustine sees the history of mankind as a struggle between the City of Man and the City of God, "two cities have been formed by two loves: the earthly by the love of self, even to the contempt of God; the heavenly by the love of God, even to the contempt of self."[3]

"In other words," commented Plinio, "either the world converts and faithfully reproduces the Augustinian vision of the 'City of God,' where each nation takes the love of God to the point of renouncing everything that harms other nations; or otherwise the world will be that city of the devil where everyone takes love of self to the point of forgetting about God."[4]

Thus we see the golden thread of good and the black thread of evil running all through the fabric of the history of mankind, sometimes side by side as in a race, sometimes intertwined as in a struggle, sometimes forming beautiful embroideries where the dark only enhances the light. Yet at other times, the black is so dense and chaotic that the gold seems to disappear. Then the fabric looks like one big black smear, with only faint glimmers of the underlying gold.

"Steps of God"

At such times, God has often intervened in history through secondary causes on the side of the "golden thread." Plinio marveled at what he called God's exceptional "steps" into history, and often spoke of them.

In the Old Testament, before the coming of Christ and the foundation of the Church, God intervened many a time such as when He sent Moses to His people long oppressed in Egypt, leading the Jews towards the Promised Land and granting them His written law, or sending Gideon to Israel threatened by the Madianites, and so on.

Of course, His greatest "step" into history was when He Himself, in the Person of God the Son, took on our flesh, was born of the Virgin Mary and redeemed us on Calvary, establishing His Holy Catholic Church to show us the way to salvation.[5]

Ever since, wherever the golden thread of the Church was woven, there was also the black thread of the Serpent harassing her with heresies, schisms and dissention. The Church never ceased to produce Saints and wise, providential people with the special vocation to fight the errors and evil of the times. For instance, as Cardinal Charles Journet points out, there have been people like a Saint Athanasius, a Saint Ambrose, a Saint Augustine, a Saint Thomas Aquinas, a Saint Catherine of Siena, a Saint Joan of Arc, a Saint Ignatius Loyola, and innumerable others with the mission to alert, inform and act.

Common to all of these persons has been clarity of vision, with the capacity to assess the totality of the evil in question; uncommon perspicacity to choose the best means to combat the particular evil; and an ardent charity and combative resolve to accomplish the task. To "counter" is their unpopular charism, and God equips them for the enterprise.

The twentieth century, which was to be one of the bloodiest, opened with a Saint Pius X who saw clearly, warned repeatedly, and acted tirelessly to "counter" what he called the great heresy of "Modernism" threatening the Church.

In the middle of bloody World War I a mighty "step" of God occurred when in 1917 He sent His own Mother to three little shepherds in Fatima, Portugal, to warn of wars and cataclysms in case the world did not do penance for its many crimes.

There has also been the initiative of many faithful sons and daughters of the Church, who, through action or writings, "countered" the evil onslaught.

Such was the case of a little book about to be given to the world through the pen of such a son.

A book called "prophetic"

In 1959, Plinio put into words all that he had been given to see and understand about the great crisis engulfing the Christian West. Joining his wide knowledge of history to his profound Catholicity and brilliant insight, he wrote *Revolution and Counter-Revolution*.

First published in *Catolicismo*, and then printed in book form, *Revolution and Counter-Revolution* has gone through numerous printings in several languages and made the rounds of the world.

In the back of the American edition, among other letters of commendation of writers, historians and ecclesiastical personages, is one from the renowned canon lawyer, Fr. Anastasio Gutiérrez, in which he calls the book ". . .a prophetic work in the best sense of the word."[6]

Revolution and Counter-Revolution is truly a "prophetic" work not just because it embraces a grand scenario, and defines, perhaps as no other, the totality of the modern day predicament, tracing it back to its origins at the end of the Middle Ages, and through the subsequent Protestant, French, Communist and Anarchical Revolutions, but most importantly because it shows how to counter this evil process.

Pope Pius XII alludes to a subtle and mysterious enemy, a destructive process, *"It is to be found everywhere and among everyone; it can be both violent and astute. In these last centuries, it has attempted to disintegrate the intellectual, moral, and social unity in the mysterious organism of Christ."*[7]

Revolution and Counter-Revolution has been translated into nine languages and spread throughout the world. Pictured above is the newest American edition.

Plinio calls this organized evil the "Revolution" with a capital "R." In his opinion it is the greatest attempt ever to subvert God's natural law and universal order.

Sensual in that it promotes a revolt against the moral order, and egalitarian in that it incites a revolt against all hierarchy, "...*the Revolution was born from an explosion of disorderly passions that is leading to the total destruction of temporal society, the complete subversion of the moral order, and the denial of God.*"[8]

The book not only alerts the present generation to a global ill, but also points to the means to "counter" this generalized seduction, placing in the hand of the reader a golden key that can be used to find the way out of the dark room of today's neo-pagan culture, thus calling for a Counter-Revolution. "If the Revolution is disorder, the Counter-Revolution is the restoration of order."[9]

Revolution and Counter-Revolution is the work of a man who was given to see the magnitude, malice, and subtlety of an evil that could only have been conceived by a perverted angelic mind, a mind so cunning that it ensnared many generations without their perceiving it. Thus, to perceive and understand how the Revolution acts, takes not only intellectual application but also a special help of God's grace.

Revolution and Counter-Revolution is a pearl of great price given to our era and not easily grasped, unless studied in depth. But it contains the answer. As in lores of old, it's there for those ready to seek it and to wield the sword it offers to cut the chains of today's subtle, but real enslavements.

Revolution and Counter-Revolution contains, as it were, the special charisma of Plinio and his group, that particular "vocation" to see, judge and act in order to counter the evils of today, and to work for the restoration of the only perfect social order that can exist, the Kingdom of Christ on earth.

Having put his vision on paper, Plinio was now ready to launch a movement and give it official status.

Notes

1. J. Ratzinger, *La théologie de l'histoire de saint Bonaventure*, Fr. Tr. (Paris, Presses Universitaires de France, 1988), p. 1.

2. Meditation on "The Two Standards," *Manresa: or the Spiritual Exercises of St. Ignatius, for general use*, (New York: The Catholic Publication Society, n.d.), p. 166.

3. St. Augustine, *The City of God*, Marcus Dods, trans., in Philip Schaff, ed., *A Select Library of the Nicene and Post-Nicene Fathers of the Christian Church*, (Grand Rapids, Mich.: Wm. B. Eerdmans Publishing Company, n.d.), vol. II, (*St. Augustine's: City of God* and *Christian Doctrine*), book XIV, chap. 28, http://www.ccel.org/ccel/schaff/npnf102.iv.XIV.28.html.

4. Plinio Corrêa de Oliveira, "Um remédio que agravará o mal," *O Legionário*, # 491, Feb. 8, 1942.

5. Cf. Matt. 16:18.

6. Plinio Corrêa de Oliveira, *Revolution and Counter-Revolution*, pp. 186-187.

7. Pope Pius XII, Allocution to the Union of Men of the Italian Catholic Action, Oct. 12, 1952, *Discorsi e radiomessagi di Sua Santità Pio XII*, (Vatican: Tipografia Poliglotta Vaticana, 1953), vol. 14, p. 359.

8. Ibid., p. 114.

9. Ibid., p. 75.

CHAPTER 20
Tradition, Family and Property

"Respect and veneration for tradition, for the family and for property was always a fundamental condition to the normal life of nations. Since time untold, such principles were the universal consensus. . . Almost suddenly, under the impulse of mysterious factors, everything began to change. . ."

—Um Homem, Uma Obra, Uma Gesta

In 1953, *Catolicismo* began to promote an annual week-long seminar, which after 1961 had swelled in attendance enough to be called "Latin American Congress of *Catolicismo*" with four hundred participants from Brazil, Argentina, Chile and other South American countries.

The presence of attendees from Argentina, Chile and other countries had been the result of the enthusiastic efforts of veterans and new members of *Catolicismo* to locate kindred spirits throughout South America. In Argentina they met an excellent group of young men of the magazine *Cruzada*, and in Chile another conservative Catholic group of young men, which later, under the inspiration of *Catolicismo*, launched the magazine *Fiducia*.

All three groups felt such kinship that they knew theirs was one family of souls in Christ. In 1960, feeling the need to give legal status to the *Catolicismo* Group, the Brazilian Society for the Defense of Tradition, Family and Property was officially created. This title indicated the three main objectives of the organization in direct opposition to the Communist ideology, which abhors tradition, undermines the family, confiscates private property and discourages private enterprise, thus compromising a true Christian civilization.

In time, the ideals of Tradition, Family and Property

The launching of a street campaign against socialist land reform in downtown São Paulo, Brazil.

would expand to Uruguay, Colombia, Ecuador, Peru, Venezuela, Bolivia, Spain, Portugal, the United States, Canada and France, and later to all five continents.

Nature of the new organization

As Plinio's spiritual life matured, he had felt the calling to remain single and celibate so as to dedicate his whole person and entire available time to the Catholic cause.

He had not always thought thus.

One day, while tidying papers on her son's desk, Dona Lucilia found a note from a young woman behind a small commemorative plaque of Plinio's First Communion.

"Son, what is this?" she inquired with a knowing look, and a half smile.

"Oh, Mamãe, it's nothing."

"But it's a note from a young woman. . ."

"Well, one day I may marry like everyone else, Mamãe. She seemed suitable, from a good family, so I sent her a book. This is a note thanking me for it. But it is all finished. I forgot it was there."

With time, the calling to a consecrated life as a lay apostle in the world grew ever clearer, and when he founded the Brazilian TFP, it was well defined. In his chivalrous mind and soul, Plinio longed to found a group reminiscent of the chivalry of old, with the same principles of selfless dedication to the defense of God's rights, only adapted to modern-day needs.

Though the TFPs have always included married members, and a large number of supporters and friends of both genders and from all walks of life, their full-time volunteer core consists of men, many of whom have chosen a celibate life, totally consecrated to the fight against the Revolution.

Plinio with hundreds of TFP members, family and friends standing outside the Cathedral of São Paulo after a solemn Mass celebrated for the victims of Communism.

This was partly due to the TFP's nature, poised to address so many of today's moral debates head on. Plinio was always too much of a gentleman to ask women to take certain issues "to the street" on a regular basis, as we shall see.

As an organization, the TFPs fall under what Canon Law defines as private associations of lay persons, established and ruled by themselves, and subjected in matters of faith, morals and discipline to the normal vigilance that the Church exercises over all the faithful.[1]

Though grounded in the Divine Magisterium of the Catholic Church and drawing their inspiration from her teachings, the TFPs were established as "lay apostolates" in direct response to Plinio's inner call to work for the interests of the Church and Christian Civilization in the world.

Gradually, many other autonomous sister TFPs were founded around the world. The American TFP began its activities in 1973.

Notes

1. Cf. Vatican Council II, Decree *Apostolicam Actuositatem* on the Apostolate of the Laity, Nov. 18, 1965, no.19.

CHAPTER 21
Illness and a Mother's "Smile"

"The luminous moments supply the great ideal.
The sorrowful moments conquer the great ideal."

—*Plinio Corrêa de Oliveira*

I look ill, mused Plinio, *I can't believe no one has noticed.* He thought this as he watched the premiere of a film shot at the occasion of a solemn Mass offered by the TFP for the victims of Communism on November 5, 1967.

Analyzing himself in the movie, and realizing how run-down he looked, he had the first premonition that something was seriously amiss with his health.

Shortly after, an abscess appeared on his right foot, the pain forcing him to use a cane to move around the house. Still, he wanted to keep his condition from his mother, and left the cane when walking to join her for dinner. One day, as he made his way to the dining room, he slipped in the hallway and fell to the floor.

"Dr. Plinio," exclaimed a maid as she attempted to help him, "you can't continue to keep this from your mother."

"No, I don't want her to know," he said emphatically.

"Even now?"

"Yes, I must be the judge of that," he finished as he regained his footing.

The next day he consulted a doctor. The laboratory exams revealed a severe diabetic crisis. He was subjected to total rest, a strict diet and drugs to try to arrest the ravages of the disease. His condition was further aggravated by gangrene in his right foot.

The doctors tried to save the limb, but eventually two toes were amputated.

Laid up in bed, and facing for the first time a crippling illness, a trial raged in his soul. He had founded the Brazilian TFP a few years before, and several circumstances made him certain that Providence had destined the organization for a large work in Brazil at the service of Christian Civilization.

On the other hand, given the uncertainty of the medical prognostic, he was just as sure that, were he to die, his work, which was just beginning to prosper, would come to naught. Every fiber of his being begged to carry this work ahead for the glory of Our Lord and Our Lady, yet his hopes and aspirations were now uncertain.

It was a dark time for Plinio. Many a time he had spoken of these "dark nights" where God tries us against that which He seems to ask of us. As with Abraham, God calls on us to do something, but then seems to remove the very means of accomplishing it. *Lord what shall You have me do*, is the perplexed cry.

A "smile" from across the sea

Back in the days at the Colégio São Luis, Plinio had been acquainted with the devotion of the Mother of Good Counsel where a beautiful copy of the image hung in the chapel of the school.

Shortly before his illness, Plinio had read the historical account of the Virgin of Good Counsel, by Msgr. Georges F. Dillon, the fascinating story of the small miraculous fresco of this invocation in Genazzano, Italy. The fresco depicts the Mother of God with her Infant Son affectionately hugging her neck.

Back in the fifteenth century, the icon was venerated in

a church in Albania. Then the country was fighting Islam and had the leadership of Scanderberg, a fearless warrior who prayed before Our Lady's image prior to his battles.

While this great warrior lived, Albania was free, but as soon as he died the resistance buckled and the Muslims took over.

One day while two of Scanderberg's former soldiers, Georgio and DeSclavis, prayed before the fresco, begging Our Lady to help their plight, the image was suddenly enveloped in light and detaching itself from the wall made its way to the sea. With eyes fixed on the refulgent Madonna, the two men followed her over the Adriatic, which solidified under their feet. On arriving in Rome, they lost sight of the painting.

Some time later, rumors began to circulate about a miraculous occurrence involving a fresco in the nearby town of Genazzano. Georgio and DeSclavis immediately knew it was their "Virgin" and made their way there. They found the fresco resting above a newly constructed altar just added to the local church.

This altar had been built at the insistence of a pious eighty-year-old widow of some means known as Petruccia. She had been granted a vision in which Our Lady asked her to carry out this work. Petruccia tried to raise funds but when the population's response was insufficient, she exhausted her own personal patrimony, which still came up short. Despite the chidings of some of the inhabitants of Genazzano, Petruccia never wavered in her resolve.

On April 25, 1467, hearing the strains of heavenly music, the people of Genazzano looked up to see a brilliant cloud approaching their town. Slowly, before their astonished eyes, a small fresco emerged and went to rest just above Petruccia's unfinished altar. Needless to say, the altar was

Our Lady of Good Counsel of Genazzano became one of the main devotions of Plinio in his late adult life after having received a significant grace which he always referred to as "the grace of Genazzano."

quickly completed.

Georgio and DeSclavis settled in Genazzano, raised families and died by their Madonna.

The fresco is there to this day. A plaque at the shrine from Albanian pilgrims begs Our Lady to return to them.

Plinio's sense of reality and of history always looked for the seal of authenticity and the Church's approval on such wonderful, miraculous occurrences. But once the authenticity of an account was determined, his sense of faith rejoiced. In the case of the story of the fresco of Genazzano, its historicity is undeniable and the approval of the Church dates several centuries back, with even Popes visiting the site, including Blessed Pope Pius IX.

Plinio was deeply moved by the details of this story and made the devotion to Our Lady of Good Counsel of Genazzano his own.

Now, there were whisperings outside his sick room. A friend of Plinio had just returned from Italy, and had brought back a replica of the Virgin of Genazzano.

As the image was brought into him, once again, as in the days of his childhood before the statue of Our Lady Help of Christians, Plinio had the strong impression that Our Lady looked at him tenderly and smiled, promising him that he would not die without fulfilling his mission. A great sweetness flooded his soul, and from that day, this conviction never left him.

A painting of Dona Lucilia, Plinio's mother, offered to him as a gift after her death in 1968.

CHAPTER 22
Closing of an Admirable Life

"In the evening of life, we shall be judged according to love"

—St. John of the Cross

As Plinio emerged from his ordeal, he knew his mother's life was closing, and he braced for the separation.

His father had passed away in 1961, and for the last seven years he had been his mother's sole support and companion.

As Dona Lucilia approached her ninety-second birthday in 1968, Plinio was grateful for her long life. She had been the great constant in his life.

She had spent her days in the atmosphere of the home, had suffered and prayed through life's challenges, always steady, faithful, serene, dispensing goodness to all she came across, faithful to her calling of wife and mother, while her son wielded the "sword" in defense of Christian Civilization. Humanly speaking, they were everything to each other.

No one knew him or loved him like she did. Aware of her son's special gifts and calling, her motherly heart kept a life-long vigil for his welfare of body and soul. "Wherever my heart goes, you go inside,"[1] she once wrote to him.

"Tell me where Plinio is. . ."

Once, he traveled to Europe but kept the information from her so she would not worry. He had given her to understand he was going to Rio de Janeiro, a true statement, as he had to travel to that city to board an international flight.

After a few days, she suddenly inquired of a relative,

"Tell me where Plinio [really] is. My heart searches for

him everywhere and cannot find him."

After a long separation, when she finally met him at the door of their apartment, her joy was boundless. But after hugs, kisses and blessings, she pushed him gently away and looked him over gravely. After a long moment, she said with relief, "My son, you are always the same."

Once more Plinio marveled at her ever-vigilant love, making sure the seductions and lures of travel had not harmed him.

Goodness

Plinio always spoke of her all-enveloping goodness, which only increased with age. It was the rose in the garden of her many virtues. During Plinio's diabetic crisis, many young men of the organization visited him at home, and had the opportunity to meet and visit with his mother as well. A few took turns in the lobby answering phones and taking messages. Ever the attentive hostess, Dona Lucilia often invited these young men in, entertained them, asked about their interests, and offered them tea and cookies. All attest that stepping into the circle of her influence was like entering a hallowed atmosphere.

Plinio had noticed that these young men came into his office in high spirits. After learning that she was taking these young visitors "under her wing," he understood whence the contentment. After all, he had been subjected to this "diet" of goodness his whole life. He had always thought that her maternal instinct was too great for just two children. He was now glad and grateful to see her surrounded by young souls, thus fulfilling in some measure her great wish to reach out to many.

She was also selfless to the point of heroism.

One day, coming home late from a day of work, Plinio

looked into her bedroom but did not see her on her bed.

"Plinio, is that you, my son?" came her voice from somewhere near the floor.

Alarmed, he stepped into the room to find her lying on the floor beside her bed. She had fallen and was too advanced in years to help herself.

"Mamãe!" he exclaimed as he bent down to her. He knew she must have been lying there for hours.

Yet her first words to him were,

"Oh, *filhão*,[2] how was your day?"

To the end she was the traditional lady she had always been. Attractive in her youth, in her old age she was beautifully enveloped in that atmosphere of sweet, noble dignity she had created. This can be glimpsed in her last photographs taken only a month before her death. Her life was now drawing to a close with that same calm serenity, and steadfast faith.

A great sign of the Cross

Knowing that the condition of Dona Lucilia's heart was delicate, Plinio had managed to keep his own ordeal, illness and amputation from her.

Suddenly, on April 20th, her condition took a turn for the worse. She began to breathe with difficulty, though remaining calm and serene, full of faith and confident in God's care of her.

"She walked toward the shadows of death in all serenity," Plinio would say.

A good friend, Doctor Duncan, assisted her in her home in her last illness.

On the morning of April 21, the day before her birthday, the assistant nurse entered Plinio's room saying,

"Come quickly, Sir, Dona Lucilia nears the end. . . "

Plinio reached for his crutches and made his way down the hall. When he entered her room, she had just breathed her last. Bowing his head, he wept torrents, repeating over and over,

"Mamãe taught me to love the Catholic Church. . ."

It was a great pain for him to have missed her last breath, and he offered this disappointment to God, just as he was certain she had offered up this last sacrifice of the absence of her beloved "Filhão" at that supreme moment.

Later, Dr. Duncan described her passing:

"On the morning of April 21, she was lucid, her eyes open, and perfectly aware of the great moment approaching, she raised her hand to her forehead, made a great sign of the cross, and fell gently asleep in the Lord."

It was the day before her birthday.

Plinio would later comment how, to him, this was as if she finished the "circle" of her life just as she had always done everything else, calmly, faithfully, and completely—without even overlapping the lines.

"Blessed are the dead who die in the Lord." (Apoc. 14:13)

Notes:

1. Letter dated July 18, 1952 from Dona Lucilia to Plinio who was traveling in Europe.

2. "*Filhão*" would translate as "my big son," Dona Lucilia's affectionate term for Plinio.

CHAPTER 23
The Big Bad Wolf

"And then came the big bad wolf. And he huffed, and he puffed, and he huffed and he puffed and he blew the house down. . ."

—*Every Parent*

After that first, prolonged bout of tears at his mother's passing, Plinio was never seen to weep in public again over her loss.

Still, those who knew him knew the immensity of his grief and marveled at his fortitude as his activity on behalf of his country's interests continued undeterred. He now bravely turned his face to the grim specter of Communism threatening his country.

An old fiend
Why do classics such as the *Three Little Pigs* and *Little Red Riding Hood* have such timeless appeal? Generation after generation, wide-eyed children listen to the drama of Fifer, Fiddler and Practical, struggling to live a peaceful life around a prowling wolf. And legions of children never tire of the story of unsuspecting little Red Riding Hood picking flowers and strolling through the woods in the company of a scheming beast.

Whence the enduring power of these simple stories? Could the genius of their authors have essentially captured the ongoing drama of the Garden of Eden, hence their long-term appeal?

Happy-go-lucky Fifers, idle Fiddlers, honest Practical homebuilders, and unsuspecting Little Red Riding Hoods, have forever been the dark objective of the same fiend that ensnared Eve and deceived Adam. Throughout history, he has put on multiple cloaks, taken various forms, and worn myriad costumes. Yet, the spirit of chaos, death and destruction invariably reveals the presence of the enemy of mankind.

One of the great beasts of our era was a Red Wolf predicted in the beginning of the twentieth century by the Mother of God herself.

Again, the year was 1917 and the month was May as three little shepherds, Lucia, Francisco and Jacinta, tended their parents' sheep in a field in Fatima, Portugal. Suddenly, a light flashed through the sky and before their astonished eyes a beautiful lady appeared atop a Holm oak. Later she revealed that she was the "Lady of the Rosary." Throughout six consecutive apparitions she spoke of the need for prayer and penance, and asked for the consecration of Russia to forestall the evils coming upon the world for its innumerable crimes.

In the third apparition, Our Lady said,

". . .If they listen to my requests, Russia will con-

Above left*:* Our Lady appeared in Fatima to Lucia, Francisco and Jacinta and told them that if mankind did not convert that Russia would spread its errors throughout the world promoting wars and persecutions of the Church. In October of that same year, the Communist revolution seized power in Russia. ***Above right****:* Lenin delivering a speech.

vert and there will be peace. If not, it will spread its errors throughout the world, promoting wars and persecutions of the Church. The good will be martyred; the Holy Father will have much to suffer, and several nations will be annihilated."[1]

On November 7 of the same year, three weeks after the last apparition, a revolution led by Lenin overthrew Russia's provisional government marking the beginning of the reign of Communism in Russia. Suddenly, Our Lady's prophetic words were crystal clear.

Much more than a political party, Communism is a system of atheistic beliefs that denies God's existence, His revealed truth and consequent morality, and natural law. Thus, it seeks to destroy the family by undermining its two flanking supports: tradition and property. In a more aggressive phase, it attacks the very structure of the family by encouraging in children a sense of responsibility to the State rather than to their parents. Books such as Kravchenko's *I Chose Freedom* are great eye-opening testimonies to the grim reality of the satanic fury of Communism.

Humanity did not heed Our Lady's requests, and Communist Russia spread its errors throughout the world. In 1960, not satisfied with the succulent dish of Russia, the Eastern European nations and China, the Red Wolf turned its fangs toward another promising feast, made more enticing because it was a cohesive Catholic block—Brazil.

Lance in hand down a narrow gully

But in the case of Brazil, the very Catholicity of the land had produced a champion. This champion, long aware of the prowler, awaited it, lance in hand down the only narrow gully he knew the wolf could try.

The former Land of the Holy Cross was no easy prey for the troublemaker. Brazil had no complaint against its past kings who had treated their subjects as their own children. Brazil had one Catholic Faith, and Brazil was a land of plenty, its soil yielding up to three harvests a year. Because of this cohesion, wealth and general contentment, Communism had only a slim entrée, only one shot at subversion. And this was to play the tune of the "landless" against Brazil's long-established landowners, seeking to introduce in the latter a feeling of "guilt" for owning "so much" while their workers "only" made a regular salary. This was called Agrarian Reform, and was actually a reform of property ownership, not of agriculture.

Backed by the media, and, unfortunately, by certain leftist sectors of the Catholic clergy, a climate of agitation began to spread, giving the false impression that there was an atmosphere of unrest and discontent among the working classes in Brazil. At first covert, but increasingly overt, a campaign of Communist agitation was launched. Songs and poems such as the one below were shockingly revealing of the Communist intent:

> Lords of the land
> Prepare your shrouds. . .
> You reap from the land
> But the land belongs
> to those who work it
> Now is the time for war. . .
> The land is ours
> As much as yours. . . .
> It's grenade against grenade
> Machine gun against machine gun,
> This is a holy war! [2]

Plinio, pen in hand, and with the cooperation of Bishops Mayer and Sigaud, and the economist Luiz Mendonça de Freitas wrote another book, *Agrarian Reform, a Question of Conscience*. Basing it on the social teachings of the Church, he told the farmers that despite the "guilt trip" being laid on them, their right to their own property was fully backed by Catholic doctrine. As long as they paid a just salary to their workers, they were on the side of justice, and no power on earth could confiscate their land without violating the seventh commandment.[3] He also dispelled the socialist myth that medium and small properties are more productive than large farms, and asked the obvious question to the promoters of revolution:

"If it is property you want to distribute, why not

Plinio delivering a speech against socialist land reform, a system of land distribution applied in Communist countries with devastating results.

dip into the lands of the State which constitute
60% of undeveloped Brazil?"

Taking to the streets, and visiting farmers and ranchers
personally all across the land, TFP volunteers sold five
thousand books in twenty days. After four editions, thirty
thousand copies had been distributed, making it a national
best seller.

The Revolution, whose ultimate goal in Brazil was not
only land reform but also an urban and industrial reform
under a Communist regime, was stalled—for the moment.

Notes

1. Antonio A. Borelli and John R. Spann, *Our Lady of Fatima*, pp. 51-52.

2. Brazilian TFP, *Um Homem, Uma Obra, Uma Gesta*, p. 63.

3. Of course, in case of public necessity (for instance to build dams, roads, etc.) or public calamity (wars, epidemics, etc) it is according to natural law and Catholic doctrine for the State to exercise public domain, but it must pay just compensation to the owner of the confiscated property so as not to weaken the right of private ownership.

CHAPTER 24
Red Against Red

"For us life is not a party but a fight. Our destinies should be those of heroes and not sybarites. . . Place Christ in the center of your life. Let all your ideals converge upon Him. . . and repeat the Savior's phrase, 'Lord, I shall not refuse to work'"

—*Plinio Corrêa de Oliveira*

"**S**ir, who designed this banner?" asked a laborer of a TFP member holding a large red and gold standard in downtown São Paulo.

"It was Plinio Corrêa de Oliveira, the man who founded our organization," answered the young man obligingly.

"Wow," continued the man, contemplating the standard waving elegantly in the wind, "this man has a great soul!"

Since its beginning, the TFP struggled against a shroud of silence imposed on its activities and initiatives by the mass-media. To break this "siege," and reach the public, Plinio conceived the idea of street campaigns.

The sight of the TFP in a city's

The standard of the TFP, as idealized by Plinio, pictures a rampant lion, turned to the left, as a symbol of the fight against Communism, on a red background, with the words, Tradition, Family and Property, the basic principles of Christian Civilization.

main thoroughfares could not be missed. In 1965, Plinio with his genius for eye-catching emblems rich in symbolic meaning had designed a golden rampant lion, with a red cross on its breast, on a field of crimson as the standard or banner of the new organization. The red stood for combat, in honor of the blood of martyrs shed throughout history for the Catholic Faith. The golden lion symbolized the combative stance in defense of Christian Civilization. The lion faced the left with open claws. Under the lion, in beautiful golden letters was the logo, Tradition, Family, Property. The banner swung from a blue crossbar, which hung from a tall blue pole finishing in a golden fleur-de-lis, symbol of Our Lady and of the virtue of purity.

The red cape worn over the shoulders was also idealized by Plinio as an emblem of TFP members used specially in street campaigns.

Plinio also designed a type of red sash or cape to be worn across the chest, which had the effect of dotting the streets with red. An anonymous pamphlet once described a street campaign in downtown São Paulo in terms that although meant to be critical, betrayed admiration:

> "Medieval angels took São Paulo by storm. As if emerging from the obscure vaults of mythology, they invade the streets, dominate the squares and take up positions of attack. . . there is no denying that there is a certain timeless beauty in those standards. . ."

The TFP took to the streets every time there was a threatened Catholic principle to uphold for the good of Brazil.

Thus, they fought land reform, an issue that would resurface time and again. They also battled divorce, which threatened to destroy the Brazilian family, and abortion, its grim companion. They continued to fight the infiltration of Communism and Progressivism into the Church, which in Brazil was rampant, giving rise to "Liberation Theology." This ideology recruited part of the clergy headed by Archbishop Helder Câmara, known as the "Red Archbishop," and Bishop Pedro Cassaldáliga. Later, despite the condemnation of John Paul II, the spirit of "Liberation Theology" continued to spread in Brazil, all the while backing the violent "Landless Workers Movement" for land reform.

Plinio's group offered a relentless opposition to these machinations, always in a peaceful, legal and respectful manner. "TFP" soon became a household name.

"What are you fighting *now*?" asked a passerby of a young TFP volunteer.

The young volunteer could not help laughing aloud as he handed a pamphlet to the man. It was good to know the red

A terrorist bomb left a large gaping hole in the façade of the first TFP seat where Plinio and his group met regularly.

standard represented an opinion which people had come to expect and respect whether they agreed with it or not.

A grim salute

Brrooooorrrrm!

A nighttime explosion rocked 665 Martim Francisco. Fortunately, none of those inside were hurt.

As the powder cleared and the dust settled, the TFP members saw a gaping hole in the façade of the building. Lying on the floor amidst the wreckage was the only casualty, a small statue of Our Lady that had been with Plinio's group from the beginning, and it was shattered.

Their Marian hearts constricted at the sight. Plinio was on the spot as soon as he was notified. As he contemplated the damage, he conceived a plan.

"Let us repair the statue," he began.

"But Dr. Plinio, she is beyond repair."

Letf: A TFP member during a night vigil in front of the shrine of Our Lady Victim of Terrorists. *Right:* The damaged statue.

"I know she will never be the same, she will always have scars, but they will serve as a reminder. In reparation, I want to build a shrine in the very place the bomb exploded. But it will face the street for every passerby to see. We will call it the shrine of Our Lady Victim of Terrorists."

On December 18, 1969, the TFP inaugurated the oratory with the proper pomp and circumstance. For thirty-five years, as long as 665 Martim Francisco was under the control of the earliest members of Plinio's group, TFP volunteers took turns in maintaining a vigil of rosaries that started at 6:00 pm and ended at 6:00 am. Passersby continually stopped to join in or say a few prayers of their own. There was always an abundance of flowers before the tiny statue, mute witnesses to numberless favors.

Bombs were also placed in TFP seats in Colombia, Chile and Uruguay. Our Lady's protection was always evident as, despite the violence of these attacks, no one was ever fatally wounded.

In the streets of the world

Far from being intimidated by such tactics, the TFPs adopted street campaigns as one of their primary means of communicating with the public, a method that, though unique, has proven most effective, as word of mouth is the surest advertisement. The TFPs campaigned and continue to campaign in big downtowns, small downtowns, wealthy suburbs, middle class suburbs and poor suburbs. It is a way of meeting the "man in the street" frankly and directly, countering the slants often aired by the media.

Here in the States, from New York to New Orleans, from Washington D.C. to Los Angeles, the American TFP every so often takes to the streets to champion the cause of Christian Civilization. A few examples were the campaign for the honor of our flag in 1989, the campaign for the freedom of Lithuania in 1990, the almost continuous protests and public acts of reparation against blasphemous movies and plays

Protest on 7th Avenue in New York City against Planned Parenthood's blasphemous depiction of the Mother of God.

since 1978, the campaigns against same-sex "marriage" starting in 2004, the campaign against *The Da Vinci Code* in 2006, and numerous others.

The written word was another of Plinio's methods for alerting and informing the public of the inroads of Communism and its collateral philosophies. Besides *Catolicismo*, which in its fifty-eight years of life had done nothing but alert and inform, Plinio also wrote a syndicated column.

For twenty-two years he contributed weekly articles to *Folha de São Paulo*, the metropolis' leading newspaper. His incisive, clever and positive-provocative titles were irresistible, and his articles widely read.

Thus it was that Plinio and the TFPs kept Communism at bay, fought for the integrity of the family, spoke up for the oft-forgotten victims of Communism, spread the Fatima message, in short, did everything they could to promote the Kingdom of Christ on earth.

The American TFP during the 2010 March for Life March in Washington D.C. The TFP has participated in the March for Life since the first March for Life in 1974.

Plinio presiding over a weekly meeting at the auditorium St. Michael, Sao Paulo, Brazil.

CHAPTER 25
Son of the Church

"Life is only worth living when you find something bigger than life to die for."

—*Plinio Corrêa de Oliveira*

For once Plinio was speechless. A lump in his throat drowned the words of thanks he owed those who had just acclaimed him as "a man truly Roman, Catholic and Apostolic," during a TFP meeting.

Finally, in a husky voice he said,

"What you have called me here tonight is the only title I have ever coveted."

Learning about the Pope

From the time in Paris when as a four-year-old he debated an irreverent puppet alligator about to eat a marionette priest, Plinio had battled in favor of the Church, its hierarchy and clergy. That love, obviously seeded in his heart by grace, only increased through the years.

His love blossomed into enthusiasm when he first learned about the Pope and the Papacy in catechism class. The instruction he received solved a problem for him.

Given to reflection from a tender age, Plinio realized as a boy that he and others were not perfect. Moreover, he began to notice in himself the harsh reality of original sin at work, which required a constant struggle on his part to harness disorderly impulses within, and work to develop the opposite virtues.

As he matured, he became increasingly aware that

many people in his own circles upheld views that in a variety of points contradicted what was truthful, virtuous and good. On the other hand, he grew in admiration for his mother, as he took note of her consistent fidelity to what was true, virtuous and good.

Thus, at the same time that he noticed the capacity for deviation and error in the human heart and mind, he was puzzled as to why his mother seemed to escape this broad rule.

"If we are all fallible, and susceptible to error, how do we avoid the world ending up in chaos? And how come *Mamãe* never deviates, thus maintaining her constant order, peace and calm?"

Marvelling at Infallibility

At nine years of age Plinio learned of the dogma of Papal Infallibility in catechism class, and how the Pope cannot err whenever defining faith and morals. Immediately, Plinio saw this dogma as additional proof that the Catholic Church is divinely instituted. To his mind it was clear that the true religion, that which claimed to possess the fullness of truth, had to have a divine "guarantee" against error. Here it was, Papal Infallibility, defined as Catholic dogma by the First Vatican Council on Christ's promise to Peter, *"thou art Peter; and upon this rock I will build my church, and the gates of hell shall not prevail against it. And I will give to thee the keys of the kingdom of heaven. And whatsoever thou shalt bind upon earth, it shall be bound also in heaven: and whatsoever thou shalt loose on earth it shall be loosed in heaven." (Matt. 16: 18-19)*

At that moment, an enthusiastic love for the Holy See of Peter was born in his heart. He also understood that his mother's constancy was the result of her consistent "alignment" with the infallible teachings of Holy Mother Church.

In an article in *Folha de São Paulo*, Plinio wrote:

> "It is not with the enthusiasm of the days of my youth that I look at the Holy See today. It is with a much, much greater enthusiasm. Because, the more I live, think and gain experience, the more I love the Pope and the Papacy. . . .
>
> "I remember when in catechism class I learned of the Papacy, its divine institution, its powers and mission. My boy's heart (I was then 9 years old) swelled with admiration, love and enthusiasm. I had found the ideal to which I would dedicate my whole life. From then until now, the love of this ideal has only grown. And I ask Our Lady to help it grow more and more within me, unto my last breath."[1]

Anchored to the Divine Magisterium

All his life, Plinio submitted lovingly to the Divine Magisterium of the Church. He studied the Popes, their pronouncements, encyclicals and dogmatic definitions. He gave special attention to the social doctrine of the Church. Those teachings were his constant point of reference, and the cornerstone of his militant action as a Catholic intellectual.

Anchored to these doctrines, he was able to confront all the ideologies that attempted to seduce the masses of his century: Nazi-Fascism, Socialism, Communism, as well as the social-cultural currents that introduced customs, fashions and lifestyles contrary to those of a truly Christian civilization.

Those who knew Plinio marveled at the self-assurance of the man. He once commented in this regard:

> "Many people believe I am self-assured. Thanks be to God, I am. But do not think this self-assurance

comes from trusting my intelligence or ideas. It comes from the fact that my doctrine is the doctrine of the Holy See. For if there is one thing I am sure of in this world, it is the indestructible bond between Our Lord Jesus Christ and the Holy Roman Catholic and Apostolic See. And if you say Holy See, you mean above all the Pope."[2]

And on the same subject,

"If I did not have the certainty that there is someone infallible who will correct me if I err, I would be so afraid of erring that I would stop thinking and would be the most insecure of men."[3]

A well-informed love

On the other hand, Plinio's love and knowledge of history showed him that some Popes did not fully behave according to the sacred nature of their charge.

"*But the treasures of the Church, her divine character, her holiness, Divine Revelation, the grace of God, spiritual authority. . . are not dependent on the moral character of the agents and officers of the Church.*"[4] Our Lord Himself foretold that one of the Church's severest trials would be the presence not only of false brethren but also of rulers who would offend. Still, those do not touch the Church's intrinsic holiness.

A hard task

One of the hardest things Plinio ever felt called to do was to resist elements of the hierarchy who either gave their knowing consent to the infiltration of Communism or were led to believe that the Red Wolf could only be handled through "dialogue" and appeasement.

In Brazil, the Marxist ideology began to make inroads

into the ecclesiastical field, spearheaded by the "Red Archbishop," Dom Hélder Câmara, mentioned previously. Ironically, earlier he had been a high-ranking member of the Integralist Party, a Nazi-Fascist group. This ideological movement preached a convergence of all philosophies and religions in the so-called utopia of a "fourth humanity" to lead an "integral revolution."[5] Not a "man for all seasons," Archbishop Câmara turned coat from the self-proclaimed "right" to the budding "Catholic left" to follow the new winds of prestige.

Of course, the media spared no breath to promote the "Catholic left." In 1968, the publicity had reached such a climax, with Archbishop Câmara filling the pages of newspapers favoring the new "Movement of Liberating Moral Pressure,"[6] that great sectors of opinion in Brazil and other South American countries were scandalized.

To prove it, in July of 1968, in a memorable campaign, the TFP collected 1,600,368 signatures from all over Brazil, also signed by several archbishops and bishops, as well as Navy, Army and Government personnel, begging the Holy See to take measures against ecclesiastical subversion in Latin America.[7]

Notes

1. Plinio Corrêa de Oliveira, "A Perfeita Alegria," *Folha de S. Paulo*, Jul. 12, 1970.

2. Alejandro Ezcurra Naón, "Plinio Corrêa de Oliveira, a Igreja e o Papado: uma gesta de fidelidade ardorosa, invariável, heroica," in *Dez Anos Depois*, pp. 99-100.

3. Armando Alexandre dos Santos, "Pensador e fundador de uma escola de pensamento," in *Dez Anos Depois*, p. 324.

4. James Loughlin, *s.v.* "Alexander VI," *The Catholic Encyclopedia* (1913), http://www.newadvent.org/cathen/01289a.htm.

5. Plinio played a significant role in shooting down this idioligical movement by means of a confidential report he wrote to the Brazilian bishops denouncing its hidden errors.

6. John R. Spann and José Aloisio A. Schelini, trans., António A. Borelli Machado, coord., *Tradition Family Property: Half a Century of Epic Anticommunism*, p. 125.

7. Cf. Ibid., pp. 130-131.

For more than 30 years, TFP members campaigned throughout Brazil spreading the message of Our Lady of Fatima to all, from the wealthiest neighborhood to the poorest.

CHAPTER 26
On the Road

*"And how shall they preach unless they be sent, as it is written:
How beautiful are the feet of them that preach the gospel of
peace, of them that bring glad tidings of good things!"*

—Romans 10:15

In 1970 Plinio conceived the idea of itinerant groups of TFP members traveling all over Brazil to fight the inroads of Communism and Progressivism. This wave was fast becoming scandalous as many priests showed open support for the subversives during the student convulsions of 1966 and 1968. From several quarters news came of religious personages pushing progressive reforms in the name of Vatican II. In the eyes of many such progressives, the spirit of the Council meant eliminating altars, statues and abandoning pulpits, cassocks and habits. This "revolution" took on a new dimension under the propulsion of the movements: "IDO-C" and the "Prophetic Groups."[1]

Meanwhile, caught between that "redefinition" of Catholicism and their simple, solid Faith, Brazilians were confused and perplexed. It was then that Plinio formed what came to be known as "caravans." These were groups of TFP volunteers who took to the road in Volkswagen vans bringing informative materials, rosaries and devotionals to the faithful in street campaigns throughout the country.

As "itinerant apostles," these young men known for their faith, courage, informative talk, peaceful behavior and flawless manners visited practically every city and town of Brazil, covering a distance comparable to a hundred trips around the globe or ten journeys to the moon! Needless to say, "TFP" became extremely well-known in the country.

Of course, communist-progressivist circles could not remain quiet, and sought to harm this effort by means of slanderous rumors, trying to make the young men out to be disturbers of the peace. But though this public promotional work of the TFP went on for thirty-five years, there was never a single official complaint against it. On the contrary, 3,713 mayors, police chiefs, and other municipal authorities testified in writing to the orderly and peaceful character of the TFP caravans.

These heroic young men left the comforts of house and home for the uncertainties of the road to spread the Faith and fight Progressivism and Communism. After a while, people trusted them and approached them with questions, prayer requests, or just to talk, often providing room, board and other necessities, which made this ongoing work possible.

Alongside its work of watching, warning and educating the public on the inroads of Progressivism and Communism, the TFP also made it its mission to spread the message of Fatima.

Over the years, the caravans echoed Our Lady's call to conversion so extensively that "Fatima" and "TFP" became words spoken in the same breath in many a Brazilian town.

Remedy for a drought, and an ox for Christmas

Once, on arriving in a town in the North of Brazil, people flocked around the Volkswagen van with complaints of a long-time drought. The young men of the TFP set up their statue of Our Lady of Fatima on top of the van, and with megaphones began calling the town folk to prayer. As people crowded around, the TFP men led a rosary and other prayers to Our Lady begging her to intercede with her divine Son on behalf of the region. That night, it rained so heavily that a few people had to be rescued in boats.

Another time, a young man knocked on the door of a house selling a booklet of Fatima. Despite the fact that Christmas was fast approaching, there were no ornaments on this door. It soon creaked open and a young woman's face appeared.

"Ma'am, would you like to buy a booklet on the story of Our Lady of Fatima?"

"Oh, I would love to," answered the woman apologetically, "but I only have small change in the house, and my husband needs the money for his taxi route tomorrow."

"Well, the book only costs three dollars."

"I still cannot do it, Sir," smiled the woman, "You know, we don't even have a roast for Christmas yet. . ."

"You know Ma'am," ventured the young man confidently, "according to the great Saint Louis de Montfort, whenever we give something as small as an egg to Our Lady, she returns us an ox. I know it is a leap of faith for you to buy this book, but I guarantee you won't be sorry. This reading will bring blessings to you and your family, and Our Lady is never outdone."

A TFP member campaigns from house to house in a poor neighborhood. The number one topic of these campaigns was invariably the spreading of the message of Our Lady of Fatima.

(Of course he could have made a gift of the booklet, but he knew that if she paid for it she would read it.)

She bought the book.

Several months later, another young man of the TFP knocked on the same door. This time, the woman's face lit up, and she said,

> "Please take this story back to all your colleagues. A while back, a young man of your group offered me a booklet on the story of Our Lady of Fatima. I was really short on cash, and hesitated to buy it, as we didn't even have a roast for Christmas. He told me, 'M'am, whenever we give an egg to Our Lady she returns us an ox.' I bought the book. Shortly after, a farmer relative called saying, 'I have just killed an ox. Would you take half of it?' Did we have a Christmas!"

Plinio listened with delight to these stories and prized those young men as sons. He spoke of their heroic dedication with admiration and immense gratitude.

"I was hungry and thou gavest me to eat; I was sick and thou didst visit Me. . ."

In the Christmas season of 1970, Plinio launched a massive campaign for the collection of funds for the less fortunate. The TFP not only believed in helping the poor for the sake of Christian charity, but also as an antidote to the ever-increasing communist agitation. Thus the TFP stood with the Church in advocating mutual charity and understanding between the classes to alleviate social tension rather than violence.

> "No violence! No violence! Let the cross and charity prevail!"

TFP members bring solace and spiritual comfort to a poor area in Brazil.

"Violence is not the answer; justice and charity are the solution."

"He who gives to the poor lends to God."

As the TFP slogans seared the air of downtown São Paulo, people applauded. Public generosity was overwhelming.

The TFP and its caravans also made it a point to visit the poor neighborhoods distributing money, clothes, shoes, blankets, household utensils, toys, furniture and medicines, as well as rosaries, medals and pictures of Our Lady.

Another charitable work of the TFP young men and their "caravans" was visiting the sick and dying. To these they brought mostly an understanding ear, the assurance of prayers and mementos of Faith.

The Fatima Visitation Program

Plinio's love for Our Lady of Fatima led him to encourage TFPs worldwide to spread the Fatima message as well. As a result, and using an adaptation of the "caravan" system, countless homes in the United States are reached with the Fatima message today. This program is one of many apostolates carried out by the American TFP's *America Needs Fatima* campaign, with ten teams of TFP volunteers on the road throughout the year, and an annex Fatima Auxiliaries Program in which TFP supporters dedicate some of their time to help out in this fruitful outreach.

Notes

1. IDO-C: International Center of Information and Documentation on the Conciliar Church.

In 1969, Plinio launched a massive, months-long TFP campaign denouncing the IDO-C and the Prophetic Groups, having learned of their existence while reading the publications *Approaches* of London and *Ecclesia* of Madrid. *Approaches* denounced the activities of a huge network with international ramifications, which cleverly managed a worldwide network of progressivist propaganda. *Ecclesia* disclosed the existence of a similar, huge network that specialized in oral propaganda. This network was made up of tiny groups encysted in the Church, forming the so-called Prophetic Groups. Both IDO-C and the Prophetic Groups aimed to transform the Catholic Church into a New Church—a desacralized, demythified and egalitarian New Church placed at the service of Communism. It was during this campaign that Plinio launched the red TFP cape that so clearly identifies TFP members on campaign.

CHAPTER 27
Two Great Devotions for Our Times

"Our Lady was always the light of my life"

—*Plinio Corrêa de Oliveira*

In July 1972, six months before abortion was made legal in the U.S., and shortly before the first Southern Decadence homosexual festival in New Orleans, world newspapers published the news of the International Pilgrim Virgin statue of Our Lady of Fatima shedding tears in a church in the Crescent City.

Accompanying the news clips was a startling photo of a beautiful profile, glass eyes filled to the brim and a large teardrop poised on the tip of the delicate nose.

Subsequent investigations and scientific tests attested that the tears were human.

Always slow to give credence to extraordinary manifestations, Plinio was deeply impressed by all the particulars of this case. Besides the details and the tears, the expression of the statue specially moved him.

The fact that this statue had

The miraculous International Pilgrim Virgin Statue of Our Lady of Fatima, New Orleans, Louisiana, 1972.

been one of four carved under the direct supervision of the main seer of Fatima, Sister Lucia, doubtlessly explained her rare physiognomy. The added fact of "human tears" coursing down her cheeks added a miraculous aura.

To Plinio, these tears from a statue of Our Lady of Fatima in a world increasing the breach between itself and her requests of 1917, were one more confirmation of the truth of her message, a message that he had made his own.

He felt a great wish to see the statue and his hopes were soon fulfilled.

Plinio helps carry the International Pilgrim Virgin statue of Our Lady of Fatima during her visit to the TFP in São Paulo, Brazil in 1973.

Visiting Brazil

In 1973, with the generous permission of Mr. John Haffert, co-founder of the Blue Army, the miraculous statue traveled to Brazil, leaving a trail of enthusiasm, love and devotion wherever it went.

On May 8, 1973, Plinio and a large contingent of the TFP received the International Pilgrim Virgin at the TFP headquarters in São Paulo. It was love at first sight. To Plinio, this representation of the Mother of God had something ineffable, majestic, and deeply maternal.

The statue returned in July of 1974, this time for a pilgrimage throughout South America. Giving full support to this tour, TFP members accompanied the statue to several countries, personally witnessing its great effect on souls through its extraordinary expressiveness, something noticed by all. Though only a statue, its effect on those who approached was deep, intense and personal, working, at times, true conversions.

On that occasion, the statue was stationed for long stretches of time at the TFP headquarters in São Paulo giving Plinio ample chance to spend many meditative hours in its presence. These prayerful times led him to write the sublime article "On Pilgrimage within a Gaze," in which he enters deep into the soul of the Blessed Mother. Inspired by the sweet glass eyes looking upon him, he "sings" of her mercies as only souls in love with her and her Son are able.

By now a veteran of many battles, as well as many sufferings, Plinio took great solace in this representation of the Queen he had chosen to serve.

Not only was the statue special to him but a favorite with all in the TFP. Through the years, it served as a liaison between Mr. John Haffert and the TFP, working a bond of friendship that would endure until Mr. Haffert's death in 2001.

Whenever on pilgrimage, the statue's custodians have always been kindly willing to accompany her on visits to the several TFPs around the world, and especially to the headquarters of the American TFP.

A message from the sixteenth century

One day in 1974, a family involved with the work of the TFP walked down one of the narrow streets of historic Quito, Ecuador. Passing in front of a church, they decided to enter. Mass was under way, so father, mother and young daughter stood in back respectfully admiring the Spanish Colonial architecture and gilded detail of the artwork. Presently, the mother whispered in her daughter's ear,

"Look. What a magnificent statue!"

Following her mother's gaze, the daughter focused her eyes on a majestic, life-size statue of the Mother of God, above the main altar. In the Spanish custom, the statue was clothed in a full dress, mantle and veil, all beautifully embroidered. On Our Lady's head was a golden crown. She held the Infant Jesus—also crowned—on her left arm, and in her right hand was an abbess' crosier.

Though at least a hundred feet from the onlookers, the statue seemed to dominate the church, so majestic was Our Lady's presence.

After Mass, the visitors looked around and were again attracted to a beautiful painting on the wall depicting the same majestic Lady, only here she was shown in a white tunic and royal blue mantle studded with stars. Kneeling at her feet was a nun, also dressed in a white habit and royal blue mantle. The nun held one end of her cincture while Our Lady held the other end as if using the cord as a measuring device.

Who was the nun in blue and white?

What were she and the Queen of Heaven measuring?

Obviously, this place had a history.

On the way out, the family picked up a pamphlet illustrated with the same painting.

An astounding account emerged.

Our Lady speaks to the twentieth century

The majestic statue is venerated as Our Lady of Good Success. On the morning of February 2, 1594, the Mother of God appeared under this invocation to Mother Mariana de Jesus Torres, a Spanish nun of the Order of the Immaculate Conception.

Mother Mariana was praying for her convent then undergoing a difficult trial, when she heard her name sweetly called. Looking up, she saw a beautiful lady in an aura of light holding a precious child.

"*I am Mary of Good Success,*" spoke the lady, "*the Queen of Heaven and Earth. . . I have come from heaven to soothe your burdened heart.*"[1]

She went on to make several prophecies about the welfare of the convent through the centuries, and finished by placing the Infant Jesus in Mother Mariana's arms.

After this, Our Lady of Good Success appeared several times to Mother Mariana with astonishing prophecies about our own times. Speaking of the twentieth century in particular, she said,

> "Unbridled passions will give way to total corruption of customs because Satan will reign. . . targeting children in particular to ensure general corruption. Unhappy the children of those times! Seldom will they receive the sacraments of Baptism and Confirmation. As for the sacrament of Penance, they will confess only while attending Catholic schools, which the devil will do his utmost to destroy by means of persons of authority.
>
> "The same will occur with Holy Communion. Oh, how it hurts me to tell you that there will be many and enormous public and hidden sacrileges!
>
> "In those times, the sacrament of Extreme Unction will be largely ignored. . . Many will die without re-

Mother Mariana de Jesus Torres.

ceiving it, being thereby deprived of innumerable graces, consolation, and strength in the great leap from time to eternity."

"The sacrament of Matrimony, which symbolizes the union of Christ with the Church, will be thoroughly attacked and profaned. Masonry, then reigning, will implement iniquitous laws aimed at extinguishing this sacrament. They will make it easy for all to live in sin, thus multiplying the birth of illegitimate children. . .

"Secular education will contribute to a scarcity of priestly and religious vocations.

"The Sacrament of Holy Orders will be ridiculed, oppressed, and despised. . . The devil will work to persecute the ministers of the Lord in every way, working with baneful cunning to destroy the spirit of their vocation and corrupting many. Those who will thus scandalize the Christian flock will bring upon all priests the hatred of bad Christians and the enemies of the One, Holy, Roman, Catholic and Apostolic Church. . .

"At the end of the nineteenth century and throughout a great part of the twentieth, many heresies will be propagated in these lands. . .

"The small number of souls who will secretly safeguard the treasure of Faith and virtues will suffer. . .

"To be delivered from the slavery of these heresies, those whom the merciful love of my Son has destined for this restoration will need great willpower, perseverance, courage and confidence in God. To try the faith and trust of these just ones, there will be times when all will seem lost and paralyzed. It will then be the happy beginning of the complete restoration...

"In those times the atmosphere will be saturated with the spirit of impurity which, like a filthy sea, will engulf the streets and public places with incredible license. . . Innocence will scarcely be found in children, or modesty in women. . . .

"There shall be scarcely any virgin souls in the world. The delicate flower of virginity will seek refuge in the cloisters... Without virginity, fire from heaven will be needed to purify these lands...

"Sects, having permeated all social classes, will find ways of introducing themselves into the very heart of homes to corrupt the innocence of children...

"Religious communities will remain to sustain the church and work with courage for the salvation of souls... The secular clergy will fall far short of what is expected of them because they will not pursue their sacred duty. Losing the divine compass, they will stray from the way of priestly ministry mapped out for them by God and will become devoted to money, seeking it too earnestly.

"Pray constantly, implore tirelessly, and weep bitter tears in the seclusion of your heart, beseeching the Eucharistic Heart of my most holy Son to take pity on His ministers and to end as soon as possible these unhappy times by sending to His Church the Prelate who shall restore the spirit of her priests."[2]

Needless to say, Plinio was deeply impressed by these predictions, the fulfillment of which, alas, he had witnessed from the days of his youth.

Again, as with Fatima, the devotion to Our Lady of Good

Success (approved by the Church since the seventeenth century), found an echo in his soul.

The statue

In one of the apparitions, Mary Most Holy asked Mother Mariana to order a life-size statue of herself made. It was to occupy the place in the choir where the mother abbess normally sits, from whence our Lady wished to rule her convent. She asked for a crosier to be placed in her right hand as a sign of her authority as superior, along with the keys of the convent so she might defend the establishment against evil intentions in the centuries to come.

It was at this juncture that the holy nun removed her cincture for an accurate measurement. Our Lady graciously took one end of the cord and put it to her forehead, while Mother Mariana stretched the other to the Blessed Virgin's feet. The cord was too short, a small matter for the heavenly visitor, who immediately caused it to grow to the required length.

Our Lady named the artist whom she wished to carry out this work, Francisco del Castillo, a pious, God-fearing

Statue of Our Lady of Good Success, Quito, Ecuador.

man, and consummate sculptor. On hearing that the Mother of God herself had appointed him, del Castillo was overwhelmed by the honor and refused payment.

When the statue had been carved, the sculptor embarked on a trip to procure the finest materials to finish the face. At this juncture, Our Lady again appeared to Mother Mariana, accompanied by a host of angels who completed the work, so that when the artist returned, sinking to his knees he exclaimed in awe that the finished statue was not the work of his hands.

At the command of her superiors, Mother Mariana left a full account of her life. Hers was a life of extraordinary virtue, prayer and penance. She not only had many visions, and received innumerable favors from God, but was given the particular mission to offer her sufferings for the twentieth century.

Plinio, always deeply moved by the concept of the Communion of Saints, was especially interested in the life of a nun whose particular mission was to pray for his epoch. He humbly attributed the graces that had enabled him to carry out his own counter-revolutionary work to the prayers and sufferings of such hidden souls.

Several times he mentioned that when, by God's grace, he entered heaven, he would like to kiss the feet of all those who prayed so that he might have the courage to pick up his cross.

Notes

1. Michelle Taylor, "A Victim for the 20th century," *Crusade Magazine*, Nov.-Dec., 1998, p. 14.

2. Ibid., p. 23.

CHAPTER 28
Intellectual and Man of Action

"Contemplate and give to others
the fruits of your contemplation."

—*Motto of the Dominican Order*

One day in the early 80's a young Brazilian history teacher contacted a member of the TFP asking to borrow the group's collection of *O Legionário*. This young man was a self-labeled moderate leftist, and though he respected the TFP and its founder, was by no means a sympathizer or follower of Plinio Corrêa de Oliveira.

The young teacher was then working on a master's thesis on Brazilian Catholic Conservatism in the 20th century. He planned to base the work on the magazines of three main Catholic organizations, Plinio's group included.

In a few weeks he completed his research of the first two publications. He then focused on the TFP, expecting to also finish in a few weeks. He was in for a surprise.

Right at the onset, the sheer volume of material astounded him. To begin, the books of the TFP, most of them from the pen of Plinio Corrêa de Oliveira, were numerous, their subjects dealing with religion, politics, sociology, philosophy, psychology, the arts, general culture, etc.

Then there was another surprise. These books were not just theoretical, written by intellectuals for intellectuals. They were written with the intention of informing, alerting, convincing and influencing the general public, always with a clear ideological goal in mind. In a word, they were books designed to inspire action. In fact, each of those books had been effective in influencing and modifying events at the time in which they were published.

The young teacher systematically read all the TFP books published to date. Then he delved into five hundred of Plinio's articles published through the years in *Folha de São Paulo*. Next, he researched *Catolicismo's* numerous essays, and was finally convinced that to understand the TFP completely, he must look into its origins in *O Legionário*, which Plinio had directed from 1933 to 1947. Here he researched about four hundred articles.

The teacher was so impressed by Plinio's amplitude of thought, and extraordinary political sense that he decided to reformulate his thesis. He would no longer address Brazilian traditional Catholicism in general, but the "TFP Phenomenon."

He now had to justify this change before the professor who was advising him on his thesis.

"How can you change your work mid-course?" was the professor's reaction. "Such a thesis requires amplitude. How can a single man, and still alive, be enough 'subject' for a thesis?"

The young man had no difficulty explaining.

"Professor, here are my reasons:

1. The amplitude of this man's written works: numerous books, and over two thousand articles.

2. Because his work, beginning in 1928, embraces a period of almost sixty years.

3. Because, of all researched authors, Plinio Corrêa de Oliveira is the only one who, in all those years, walked a straight line. He was never influenced by ideological "fads" but was always faithful to the same ideological and religious principles adopted in his youth.

4. Because of all the conservative intellectuals, he is the only one who is not merely an intellectual, but also a man of action. Whether popular or unpopular, he extended his action throughout the world.

5. Because he is different from other conservative intellectuals. While these quote and repeat with little variation the teachings of the great masters of traditionalist thought in the 19th century, and cite each other often, Plinio Corrêa de Oliveira's thought is original and he quotes very little. He almost always quotes from the official Magisterium of the Church. Everything else is the fruit of his thought and intellectual labor."

The advisor, a European and therefore not completely up to par on Brazilian affairs, asked to see the vast documentation on which the young teacher intended to base his thesis. After two weeks, he returned everything saying,

> "I approve your thesis. I find it incredible that I, who have frequented the Brazilian academic world for years, still don't know in depth a man of this intellectual magnitude."

The teacher went ahead with his thesis, which he titled, *"The TFP Phenomenon"* with the subtitle, *"A Crusader of the 20th Century."*[1]

Universal man

In fact, for Plinio, "thought and action" were intimately united. And because his thought was rooted in faith and wisdom, his action was far reaching, and obtained solid results.

"One day our little group will spread all over the world," Plinio had said to his friends in the days of the "catacombs."

As the 80's approached, it had become a fact. The Brazilian TFP having been created in 1960, within years TFPs started appearing first in South America, then Europe and North America. They were soon to reach South Africa, Australia and the Philippines.

Though legally autonomous, the different TFPs drew their inspiration from Plinio, seeking his advice in letters, and by way of the phone and personal visits.

Plinio made himself available to all, many times receiving visitors until late in the day.

There were also yearly international conferences attracting TFP members from all over the world, as well as supporters and friends. These conferences were lively affairs, with informative, motivating talks and skits, and a great social opportunity where friends could meet around a shared ideal and love for the faith. The highlight was always a talk by Plinio, who now in his seventies, still deliv-

Plinio speaks to more than 2,000 participants of an international conference of friends and supporters of the TFPs around the world.

ered in an amazingly youthful voice. His never-waning charm, brilliance and fire inspired all.

"Plinio," his father had often said to him, "a true orator is not one who speaks 'difficult,' but one who makes the 'difficult' accessible to all."

Another invaluable piece of advice was from his mother,

"Plinio, whenever you begin to think that you should close a talk, your audience will already have been thinking it for a while. Don't overextend yourself. Sometimes, less is more."

By applying these two valuable tips to his natural talent, he interested young and old alike. To make history, philosophy, theology and Catholic doctrine comprehensible and attractive to ages 8 to 80 was his specialty.

As one of the TFP's activities was working with the youth, many times Plinio found himself lecturing twelve to eighteen-year-olds with the same ease as adults, and with the same result: an enthralled audience.

Moreover, no nationality was a closed book to him. He had a true charisma to "decipher" the characteristics of each nation with an ease that astounded everyone. A truly universal man, he penetrated the mentality of the American, the European or the Asian with the same ease. His insights into their characteristics, at times, left people open-mouthed and smiling from ear to ear, as they felt perfectly "understood."

A wall of media silence with intermittent uproars

For the most part, the media's treatment of Plinio and his group was a great wall of silence, hoping to neutralize his influence by keeping his work in the dark. Thus, we again understand the above professor's remark about not knowing in depth a man of such intellectual magnitude.

But the "Crusader of the 20th Century" was not a man to be contained, and his action always hit the mark so "painfully" that many a time it goaded the reluctant media and opposing groups into a violent backlash. Veritable storms of slander were launched against the various TFPs through the years. They were accused of Nazi-Fascist tendencies (a group, which during Hitler and Mussolini's time had published 2,509 articles against the tyrants), of subversive actions, of recruiting young men for military training for violent purposes — all groundless.

Plinio refuted these accusations one by one, and never, throughout his whole career, heard a word from his detractors after such refutations.

Plinio greets a mother during a national conference for TFP supporters.

Plinio delivers a speech after the celebration of the Holy Sacrifice of the Mass for the victims of Communism in 1973.

Speaking of a particular media uproar, one person commented that such an onslaught would have been enough to topple a government.

Still, through the grace of Our Lady, the small ship with the red sails and golden lion always emerged from the smoke of such public battles, at times singed and splintered, but never beaten. It had a superb admiral who had formed his captains well.

Worldwide activity

With TFPs now in five continents, the different groups were able to address current issues worldwide. As Prof. Roberto De Mattei, author of *The Crusader of the 20th Century* puts it, "*The prominent role of the associations that followed Plinio Corrêa de Oliveira was to oppose the psychological war being waged on all continents by Communism and to counter it with the integrity of Catholic doctrine."*[2] Thus, abortion, euthanasia, divorce, socialism, communism, public blasphemy and a host of attacks on traditional customs, were confronted on a regular basis.

Two examples below will give an idea of this intellectual man of action's world effectiveness.

Countering Self-Managing Socialism

In 1981, François Mitterrand launched Self-Managing Socialism in France. Mitterrand intended this new form of socialism to have a "human face," and to become a new model for the world, symbolized by the fist holding a rose. Plinio caught on to this program and exposed its fallacy. On December 9 of that year, thanks to generous, dedicated donors, he published in *The Washington Post*, and the *Frankfurter Allgemeine Zeitung* of Frankfurt a six-page manifesto titled, *"The Double Game of French Socialism: Gradual in Strategy, Radical in Goal—What Does Self-Managing Socialism Mean for Communism: A Barrier? Or a Bridgehead?"*

In it Plinio demonstrated that the program of self-managing socialism was designed to break up society into autonomous cells not only in the industrial, commercial and rural enterprises, but also in the family, the school and all of social life. Ultimately, the "fist and the rose" carried the Marxist and Leninist utopia of a society without a system of authority to its last consequences.

After the first two publications, the massive essay appeared in another forty-two of the most important Western papers. A summary was also published in the *Reader's Digest* and in its several international editions, plus another twenty-three publications. All together, 33 million copies were distributed throughout the world.

This publication produced an avalanche of letters of support, including many from ecclesiastics. The reaction from Greenland to South Africa, and from Australia to the Americas was overwhelming, calling for new TFP foundations. After the publication of the "Message" as this manifesto came to be called, the TFPs went from thirteen to twenty-five around the world.

Self-managing socialism took a crippling blow. Mitterand's program was a total failure in France.

Lithuania

Another such action with broad international results was the worldwide campaign for the freedom of Lithuania, which amounted to a direct shot at Gorbachev's "perestroika," the successor to Mitterrand's Self-Managing Socialism.

The history of Communism with its systematic "choking" of liberty, generalized poverty, and tyranny of prisons and concentration camps had provoked a deep discontent within the populations of the communist block. The several attempts at throwing off that oppressive yoke such as the Hungarian rebellion in 1956, and that of Czechoslovakia in 1968 showed the world the truth. Though the media continued to present the Soviet empire as a towering giant, "the other 'superpower'" as it was generally called, in reality it was a putrefying system facing internal disintegration. The "superpower" drew its strength mainly from Western resources.

Much had been expected of Mitterrand's "socialism with a human face" as far as putting a new make-up on the international image of Communism.

Once the rose within the fist wilted, Mikhail Gorbachev with his new talismanic words, "perestroika" and "glasnost" stepped onto the scene.

The media was poised for Gorbachev's entrance onto the international stage in 1985, and lost no time in catapulting him to the center of events. His were the front pages of newspapers and magazines, newsrooms and TV productions, with messianic projection.

He was the man of the hour with the perfect plan for "reform" and the perfect attitude. Communism had replaced the scowl of Stalin and the frown of Brehznev with the smile of Gorbachev.

Plinio during a public conference in São Paulo, Brazil.

While "perestroika" meant "reconstruction," "glasnost" meant "transparency." Gorbachev's was a new message of *"transition from an excessively centralized management system relying on orders, to a democratic one, based on the combination of democratic centralism and self-management... It is the comprehensive development of democracy, socialist self-government, encouragement of initiative and creative endeavor, improved order and discipline, more glasnost, criticism and self-criticism in all spheres of society."*[3]

But in defending self-managing socialism, Gorbachev did nothing but echo the ideas of Lenin as he explains in his book, *Perestroika*. Also, his plan by no means included a reform of the Marxist economy:

> "I do not think the working class will support those authors who want to start making our society capitalist."[4]

Gorbachev's sly maneuver was not lost on Plinio who alerted the public:

> "Perestroika is no retreat from Communism as some may think, but rather a step toward the realization of the final goal of the Marxist-Leninist utopia."[5]

After the wall came tumbling down

On November 9, 1989 the Berlin wall came down before the astounded eyes of the world. Encouraged by this turn of events as well as Gorbachev's talks of "perestroika," many countries of the Soviet block moved for independence.

The world was about to watch the Soviet "boot" come down with (literally) crushing force on the country of Lithuania, which provided an important port for the Communist block, despite all the smiles and talk of "reconstruction" and "transparency."

On January 12, 1991, the world watched in horror as Soviet tanks moved in on the station of the Lithuanian TV as a multitude gathered to defend it. On January 13, the tanks attacked. When all was done and finished, 14 civilians had lost their lives, two crushed under the tanks and 240 left wounded. A little later, Latvia suffered a similar treatment.

On the same day, January 13, the government of Lithuania appealed to the American TFP. A letter from President Landsbergis accompanied the message. He wrote, "The responsibility for each victim will lie with Mikhail Gorbachev."

Plinio responded to the Lithuanian cry for help the same day, with words of admiration and encouragement for their heroic resistance to the "clearly Stalinist tactics that Mikhail Gorbachev and his agents are implacably applying against Lithuanian independence."[6]

On May 31, 1991, Plinio launched an international campaign collecting signatures in support of Lithuanian independence. After 130 days, 5,218,520 signatures were collected in 26 countries. The fact was registered in the 1993 edition of the *Guinness Book of Records* as the largest petition drive in history.

In the United States alone, young volunteers of the American TFP covered 180 cities in 33 states in several "caravans." In this effort, two members lost their lives in an accident while traveling through Tennessee. The eldest was a veteran member of the organization and "everybody's friend," Fred Porfilio, and the younger a new convert to the Church, Daryl Huang.

The campaign closed in October. In the end, Lithuania gained its independence, which was recognized by the Soviet Union in September 1991. But in the process, Gorbachev had relived the times of Stalin, and with it had confessed the falsehood of his "perestroika." It was his political demise.

On December 4 of the same year, a delegation of the TFP solemnly delivered the signatures, in microfilm format, to President Vytautas Landsbergis in Vilnius, capital of Lithuania. With touching gratitude, he and his administration as well as the people of Lithuania treated them as honored guests of State.

At the suggestion of President Landsbergis, the TFP delegation traveled to Moscow to deliver a written report on the TFPs' campaign to Gorbachev, which was done with a confirmation receipt from the Kremlin.

At the special session at the Lithuanian Congress celebrating the fifteenth anniversary of the independence of Lithuania, only two foreigners were invited to speak: the Ambassador of Iceland and the TFP representative, Dr. Caio Xavier da Silveira.

Notes

1. Cf. Armando Alexandre dos Santos, "Pensador e fundador de uma escola de pensamento," in *Dez Anos Depois*, pp. 313-319.

2. Roberto De Mattei, *The Crusader of the 20th Century*, p. 161.

3. Mikhail Gorbachev, *Perestroika: New Thinking for Our Country and the World*, (New York: Harper & Row, 1987), pp. 34.

4. Bill Keller, "Gorbachev Says It's Not Time for Soviet Private Property," in *The New York Times*, Nov. 17, 1989.

5. Plinio Corrêa De Oliveira, "Has Communism Died? And What About Anti-Communism?" *The Wall Street Journal*, Nov. 3, 1989, p. B58, n.1.

6. Plinio, letter to President Vytautas Landsbergis, Jan. 13, 1991.

Plinio was foremost a man of prayer. His faith was an inspiration to all who knew him.

CHAPTER 29
A Man of Prayer

"I can do all things in Him who strengthens me."

—*Philippians, 4:13*

"Dr. Plinio," spoke this writer, while visiting with him in 1985, "you will not be leaving us any time soon because God needs you."

"God needs no one. Understand me, He needs no one," he repeated.

Kind and affable, he was suddenly severe as his eyes deepened seeking to impress his conviction of this statement.

At such moments it struck home that this man's amazing appeal lay in a play of opposites that always managed to come together like the two sides of a gothic arch meeting harmoniously on high. Brilliance and profound humility. Combativity and touching kindness. Continuous action and serene calm. Shrewd as a serpent and artless as a child. Profound wisdom and utter simplicity. Society man and man of prayer. Enthusiast and friend of the cross.

It all made for something of a symphony, a grand charm, that left those who met him asking themselves, "whence the balance?"

The source was his profound prayer life that included all of his actions and thoughts.

Man of action, Plinio drew his astounding energy from a deeply contemplative life. His secretary of eighteen years, Fernando Antunez, writes, "*the fountain from which sprung all his activities and struggle on behalf of Christian Civilization. . . was a profound spiritual life of contemplation and prayer. He was a contemplative even in the heat of battle.*"[1]

Prayer in the Catholic sense

The famous treatise on prayer of Saint Teresa of Avila, *The Interior Castle*, describes the human soul as a castle with seven mansions arranged concentrically. The outer ones eventually lead to the central room where God resides. The spiritual life is a journey from mansion to mansion, from the first stages, beginning with a consistent effort to break with our sinful habits, to a sincere seeking of God's will in all we do. (This may include mansions one, two and three.)

As the soul labors to bring its will into conformity with God's will, it enters the intermediate stages, (mansions four and five) the beginnings of "infused prayer and contemplation." At this point, God begins gently to communicate Himself to the soul. The practice of virtue becomes less and less burdensome, which could be exemplified by a sailboat propelled by the wind versus rowing.

As the soul enters into a deeper and deeper union with God, it enters the last stages, (mansions six and seven) arriving at what Saint Teresa calls the "transforming union." Here, heroic virtue results, as nothing is difficult to a person in love. At this stage, contemplation is accomplished not so much by using creation to reach God, but it is a restive, yet active state in which everything is seen in God and understood through God.

According to Saint Teresa, everyone, in every state of life, is called to make the full journey. Many, indeed, pass through the first and intermediate mansions, but only a few arrive at the last phases. She ascribes this to the failure of souls to detach their hearts from the many cares of this earth and attach them primarily to God. In this she echoes Our Lord's teaching of the seed, which falls among the thorns, symbolic of the riches and pleasures of life (Luke 8:14).

It is this spiritual life "journey" that the mystic and doctor of the Church calls "prayer." [2]

Learning young

For Plinio, this was the real journey of life, and he began early.

Once when a small boy, he watched as an ant laboriously carried a leaf much bigger than itself. With the aid of a stick, he mischievously thought to tip it, but then caught himself.

"*Plinio*," he rebuked, "*instead of playing mischief with this ant, you should learn a lesson from it. Here it is, dutifully carrying a load fifty times it's size to nourish it's colony. Likewise, you should be prepared to carry the cross of your duty even when daunting.*"

And he left the ant alone.

He had already begun to walk the way of self-examination and conformity to virtue that would later cause him to teach, "*either we get a vice-grip on our defects or our defects get a vice-grip on us.*" [3]

Prayer life

All his life he walked the narrow path of honesty, of conforming to Truth, anchoring the ship of his soul to the teachings of God's mouthpiece on earth, the Divine Magisterium of the Catholic Church.

The Sacraments were his spiritual food. From his days in the Colégio São Luis, he frequented them assiduously. As soon as he could, he became a daily communicant, a practice that he maintained to the end of his life. His three great devotions were the Eucharist, Our Lady and the Vicar of Christ.

He saw the Sacramentals of the Church as spiritual helpers too, making frequent use of holy water, carrying the rosary in his pocket and wearing the miraculous medal and the brown scapular.

Again, his secretary, Fernando Antunez, writes that he began his day invariably with fifteen minutes of prayers. These were various prayers, accumulated through life, which he never ceased to offer. He explained, *"what you offer Our Lady, you never take back."*[4]

Every afternoon, Plinio rode to a church where he could pray undisturbed. *"As he sat in the car,"* Mr. Antunez writes, *"his countenance would change. He was beginning to say a long list of prayers, not least among them the Consecration to Our Lady according to the method of St. Louis Marie Grignion de Montfort. He would go on to say with remarkable piety the psalms of the Most Holy Name of Mary, the Small Office of Our Lady, perpetual novenas, prayers for the Holy Pontiff, chaplets of ejaculations and many other prayers."*[5]

Plinio also prayed three rosaries daily.

Elevation of the mind to God

But besides what we could call his "vocal prayer life," a part of Plinio seemed to "live" with God.

"What drew my attention the most," continues Mr. Antunez, *"was Dr. Plinio's capacity to elevate his mind to metaphysical themes and onto the supernatural even as he found himself in the middle of the most varied activities. This is a good definition of prayer:* Elevatio mentis a Deo.

"Whether it is in meetings on socio-political affairs, working to resolve daily problems and answer consultations, or in so many other meetings about temporal society, which he dealt with abundantly, Dr. Plinio would relate everything to religion, Our Lady, and Holy Mother Church."[6]

As an example, he was once speaking of a practical, concrete subject from which he suddenly rose to the highest spiritual considerations. Someone asked him how he managed to pass from the practical to the spiritual so effortlessly. He answered that the question should rather be how he could pass from contemplation to the practical. He explained that, without leaving the plateau of contemplation, he addressed the smallest concrete things, as do birds of prey that sometimes climb even higher to make sure of their prey on the ground.

Plinio explained the above in all simplicity, unwittingly revealing an advanced stage of prayer.

Speaking of the soul in the last stages of prayer, Saint John of the Cross, Saint Teresa's counterpart, says:

> "The soul is conscious of how all creatures, earthly and heavenly, have their life, duration and strength in Him. . . Although it is indeed aware that these things are distinct from God insofar as they have created being, nonetheless that which it understands of God, by His being all these things with infinite eminence, is such that it knows these things better in God's being than in themselves. And here lies the remarkable delight of this awakening: the soul knows creatures through God and not God through creatures."[7]

Perhaps this explains Plinio's uncanny ability to comment in depth and with profound wisdom on the full range of God's creation: from the blazing sun to the tiny ant, from the foaming ocean to a dew drop; and the many social situations, from a coronation ceremony to the proper setting of a table; as well as his ability to decipher the characters of nations, the strategies of politics, the depth of souls, and to scale the heights of doctrine.

Notes

1. Fernando Antunez, "Plinio Corrêa de Oliveira, um contemplativo," in *Dez Anos Depois*, p. 183.

2. Based on Fr. Thomas Dubay's *Fire Within*, a masterful interpretation of the method of prayer of Sts. Teresa of Avila and John of the Cross for our modern minds.

3. Plinio in many talks.

4. Fernando Antunez, "Plinio Corrêa de Oliveira, um contemplativo," in *Dez Anos Depois*, p. 184.

5. Ibid., p. 184.

6. Ibid., p. 185.

7. Fr. Thomas Dubay, S.M., *Fire Within*, p. 189.

Plinio once commented that as the Crusaders took the sword to the enemies of the Church in the battlefields, our battle today is done with ink.

CHAPTER 30
Friend of the Cross—Death

*"I have fought the good fight,
I have finished the race,
I have kept the faith."*

—*2 Timothy, 4:7*

A s every true servant of God, Plinio embraced his cross as an athlete embraces his trophies. He viewed the cross, never lacking in his life, as God's seal upon the authenticity of his mission. For him, the cross was something to "lift high," as the song proclaims.

Along with *True Devotion to Mary*, he promoted another of St. Louis de Montfort's works, *Friends of the Cross*. The Marian apostle opens this book saying,

> "Friends of the Cross, you are a group of crusaders united to fight against the world, not like those religious men and women, who leave the world for fear of being overcome, but like brave, intrepid warriors on the battlefront, refusing to retreat or even to yield an inch. Be brave. Fight with all your might."[1]

In his battle for the Church and Christian Civilization, seeking the Kingdom of Christ on earth, Plinio often found support in these words of the great saint—for battles and crosses he never lacked.

Besides the cross of living in a world defiant of God's law, Christian morality, and gracious living, Plinio had his share of persecution since the days when he published *In Defense of Catholic Action*, and the "house" came down on his head and that of his small group. Because of his Catholic stance, he suffered the cross of ostracism and misunderstanding even from those closest to him.

Then there were the intermittent grueling public uproars against his organization, always with full media coverage. This form of persecution followed him to his deathbed. There was also the cross of founding and leading the Brazilian TFP, and helping other TFPs worldwide, which required his constant and complete dedication, especially as he treated each and every TFP member as a son.

He also bore the bitter cross of disappointment and even betrayal throughout his life and to the very end, from certain friends and spiritual sons who closed ranks with those who wished him harm. He carried the cross of ill health as well, when he became severely diabetic, in 1967, and was subject to a strict diet for the rest of his life.

Victim Soul

In 1975, he made an astounding offer to God in favor of the Catholic cause, and particularly for the sanctification of the members of the TFPs. Following the example of his longtime friend, St. Thérèse of Lisieux, he offered himself as a victim in holocaust to God, for whatever He willed.

The next day, he suffered a devastating automobile accident that confined him to a wheel chair and the use of crutches for the remaining twenty years of his life. He bore this trial without complaint and continued to give of himself to all who needed him, as well as meet with every daily obligation both public and private.

Testimony of a son of the Church

As Plinio sensed the end of his life approaching, he wrote a spiritual testimony that gives us a glimpse of the fire that fueled him and the great love that moved him:

> "In the name of the Most Holy and Undivided Trinity,
> Father, Son and Holy Ghost, and of the Blessed Virgin

Mary, my Mother and Lady. Amen.

"I, Plinio Corrêa de Oliveira. . .

". . .declare that I have lived and hope to die in the Holy Roman Catholic and Apostolic Faith, which I hold with all the strength of my soul. I cannot find sufficient words to thank Our Lady for the privilege of having lived since my very first days and of dying, as I hope, in the Holy Church. To it I have always devoted, currently devote, and hope to devote until my last breath absolutely all my love. All the persons, institutions, and doctrines I have loved in the course of my life and currently love, I have loved and love solely because they were or are in accord with the Holy Church, and in the measure to which they were or are in accord with the Holy Church. Likewise, I never opposed institutions, persons, or doctrines except insofar as they were opposed to the Holy Catholic Church.

"In the same manner, I thank Our Lady—without being able to find adequate words—for the grace of having read and disseminated the Treatise of True Devotion to the Most Holy Virgin, of St. Louis Marie Grignion de Montfort, and of having consecrated myself to Her as Her perpetual slave. Our Lady was always the Light of my life and from Her clemency I hope she will continue to be my Light and my Help until the last moment of my existence.

"Again, I thank Our Lady—and with what emotion—for having granted me to be born of Dona Lucilia. I revered and loved her to the utmost of my capacity and, after her death, not a single day passed without my remembering her with unspeakable longings. Of her soul I also ask that she assist me until my last moment with her ineffable goodness. I hope to meet her in Heaven amidst the luminous cohort of souls who most specially loved Our Lady.

"I am fully conscious of having fulfilled my duty by having founded and directed my glorious and dear TFP. In spirit, I kiss the standard of the TFP that hangs in the Room of the Reign of Mary. The spiritual link that unites me to each member of the Brazilian TFP, as well as to those of the other TFPs, is such that it is impossible to mention any one in particular to express to him my affection. I ask Our Lady to bless each and every one of them. After death, I hope to be near Her, praying for all of them, thus helping them more efficaciously than in this earthly life.

"I forgive with my whole soul those who have given me cause for complaint. . .

"I have no instructions to give for the eventuality of my death; Our Lady will provide better than I.

In any event, from the depth of my soul and on my knees, I beseech each and every one to be completely devoted to Our Lady all the days of their lives. . ."[2]

A fighter to the end

In August 1995, as he put the finishing touches on a TFP statement, he lost consciousness. Diagnosed with the last stages of a severe cancer, he entered a period of semi-consciousness.

On October 3, 1995, the day then dedicated to the feast of St. Thérèse of the Child Jesus, surrounded by several of his closest friends and spiritual sons, Plinio Corrêa de Oliveira gave up his warrior soul to God.

Notes

1. St. Louis de Montfort, *A Circular Letter to the Friends of the Cross*, (Bay Shore, N.Y.: Montfort Publications, 1999), p.7.

2. "Our Lady was always the Light of my life"–Excerpts from the Sealed Testament of Plinio Corrêa de Oliveira, *Tradition, Family and Property Magazine*, Nov.-Dec., 1995, p. 33.

Epilogue

The TFP gave its founder a funeral worthy of a general. There were large representations from TFPs around the world, and for one day São Paulo witnessed a sea of red standards and red capes and a multitude of people accompanying the wooden casket to its last place of rest, the Cemetery of Our Lady of Consolation.

Lying in his coffin, he looked like one of those knights carved on top of medieval tombs, solemn, serious, serene, hands folded, a Rosary intertwined through his fingers.

As his coffin was sealed, hearts hung heavy, and tears flowed quietly.

Those of us who knew him, and whose lives he touched, grieved his passing like that of a father, friend and guide. A true beam of faith and fidelity in a century of moral chaos, he helped to light our paths, mend our ways, and, therefore give us the only peace that can grant

Plinio's funeral Mass at Nossa Senhora da Consolaçao church.

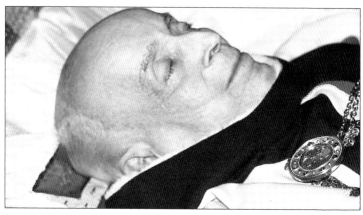

Plinio laying in state after his death on October 3, 1995.

a measure of happiness in this valley of tears—the peace of Christ from the order of Christ.

Our hearts overflow with gratitude as we now try to pass on to the next generation the golden key he placed in our hands, the key to raising our children impervious to the culture of death and alive to the kingdom of Christ on earth.

The hope that he expressed in his last testimony of continuing to aid his spiritual sons from Our Lady's side is fulfilled in the many TFPs throughout the world carrying on his work. We are especially proud of our own American TFP and its nationwide work with America Needs Fatima for which he had a special affection.

Plinio's funeral procession from the Brazilian TFP's headquarters to the cemetery Consolação on October 5, 1995.